Why Culver

The Culver Mission

Culver educates its students for leadership and responsible citizenship in society by developing and nurturing the whole individual — mind, spirit, and body — through an integrated curriculum that emphasizes the cultivation of character.

Principles

Culver is committed to the intellectual growth of all members of its community through participation in a demanding curriculum that prepares students for success in higher education. Culver's curriculum emphasizes critical thinking, problem solving, writing, research, artistic expression, and foreign language proficiency through innovative teaching methods and technologically rich classrooms. Equally important is the cultivation of those virtues that develop both a lifelong love of learning and a commitment to the responsible stewardship of knowledge.

Character development is essential to the Culver mission. For over a century the foundation of the Culver model has been an education in the classical virtues of wisdom, courage, moderation, and justice. Given that habits of mind, spirit and body develop slowly, an education in the virtues requires understanding, self-discipline, and practice. All aspects of Culver's academic, residential, extracurricular, and athletic curricula are designed to provide students with opportunities for individual growth within a carefully structured environment and provide opportunities for them to begin the difficult task of developing lifelong habits.

At Culver, leadership training is both an end in itself and the means by which students develop a sense of social responsibility. Culver Military Academy is organized around its own distinctive military system of student leadership, while Culver Girls Academy is modeled on a prefect system. With these distinctive systems of leadership, Culver's students enjoy the benefits of equal leadership opportunities in their separate residential programs, while sharing in the advantages of a coeducational program in most other areas of school life. Through the enactment of leadership ideals made possible in and through these systems, they develop confidence in their abilities to complete difficult and challenging tasks, as well as habits of inquiry and self-discipline central to an education in the virtues.

Culver is committed to the spiritual development of its students. To encourage students to take the pursuit of spiritual truth seriously, Culver provides a variety of opportunities for the exploration and expression of religious faith. To this end every student participates in a school chapel service or similar faith activity. While Culver's religious heritage is rooted in the Judeo-Christian tradition, we recognize and celebrate the rich diversity of faith and practice found among our students. The fruits of the cultivation of the spirit — a regard for the beauty of the world, a reverence for the gift of life, and a recognition of the limits of our understanding — are important components of a virtuous life.

Culver's programs in the visual and performing arts promote both aesthetic literacy and artistic practice. The arts are the common language of humanity and their study can lead to a deeper understanding of life and respect for cultural diversity. Emphasizing both theory and practice, Culver's arts programs contribute to the intellectual and personal development characteristic of an integrated approach to education and to an education in the virtues.

Culver's athletic, health, and physical education programs are an integral part of our curriculum. Participation affords a significant opportunity for the development of the virtues associated with personal integrity. While we encourage individual and team excellence, Culver's rich and varied programs are designed to present students of all skill and experience levels with opportunities to develop both a lifelong interest in sport and a lifelong regard for good sportsmanship. Culver's health and residential life curricula emphasize sound decision-making through programs that include fitness, nutrition, and respect for the body.

Left: Culver's commencement ceremony is one of its most hallowed and memorable traditions.

©2022 by Culver Academies
Culver, IN 46511
This book is sold with the understanding that neither the authors nor Culver Academies is engaged
in rendering professional services or advice by publishing this book. The author, designer, and Culver
Academies disclaim any liability, loss, or risk resulting directly or indirectly from the use or application
of any of the contents of this book.

Editors: Jeff Kenney, Kathy Lintner, and Alan Loehr
Design: Scott Adams Design Associates, New York, NY
Printing: WestCamp Press, Westerville, OH
Company and product names mentioned herein are the trademarks or registered trademarks of their
respective owners.
All rights reserved. No part of this book may be reproduced, in any form or by any means, without
permission in writing from Culver Academies.
Printed in the United States of America
First Printing November 2022
ISBN 979-8-218-09220-7

Why CULVER

A memoir by
JOHN BUXTON

FOREWORD

Education is not preparation for life; it is life itself.
                                                  — *John Dewey*

As John Buxton recounts in these pages, when he was first approached about becoming President of the Culver Academies, he did not believe he was the man for the job. He knew little of the institution and did not believe he "had the background needed to run a military school."

But, as a person and as an educator, John is committed to lifelong learning and development. And what he learned about Culver changed his life, as it has so many. This process is captured clearly and compellingly in this thoughtful and insightful volume.

As it happened, John was pursuing a Ph.D. at the time he met Culver. As he explains, "One of the reasons I had enrolled in a graduate program at age 50 was so I could link up educational theory with practice." Culver became his subject, his test case and, in many ways, his muse as he completed this work. And he brought that learning back to the school to help make it better still.

Part memoir, part history, and part exploration of pedagogical theory, this book plunges into the culture of Culver to understand what makes it work and sets it apart. In analyzing private school models — the American prep school tradition, from which he came; its precursor, the English public-school tradition; and the military model he met through Culver — John lays out the differing goals, styles, and strategies of each and the results they consequently produce.

After 30 years as a teacher, administrator, and leader at one of America's most prestigious prep schools, he becomes an ardent convert to the Culver model because of those results, embodied in the characters of the young men and women who form the school — and whom the school has formed. He and Pam, his wife and partner in this journey, are struck, again and again, by the behavior of the remarkable young people they meet through the Academies. By the strength of their values; the conscientiousness with which they internalize, protect, and pursue them; and, above all, by the right action to which they lead.

Based on his own learning, John identifies the key to this successful character-building: Aristotelian habituation, the philosopher's recognition that "We are what we repeatedly do." By giving its principles form in action, and by ingraining them through

Miles White '73, Culver Educational Foundation Chairman, is greeted at the Iron Gate on his graduation date, Monday, June 4, 1973, by Legion President, Bill Macomber '50.

purposeful and dedicated habit, Culver helps its students acquire not just skills and knowledge, but ultimately, as captured in Culver's Code of Conduct, "To place duty before self, to lead by example, and to take care of those I lead." This is why his title — "Why Culver" — is a statement, not a question.

John discusses each of the many pieces that compose the totality of Culver — CMA, CGA, Woodcraft Camp, the Summer School, the Black Horse Troop, the Naval School, the Aviation School — and understands how they each contribute to creating the Culver experience and what each means to the unique culture of the institution. Through his excellence as a professional educator and his commitment to the institution he led and the young people in its charge, as Head of Schools, John helped to not just preserve that culture, but to strengthen and enhance it, navigating the many changes continuously taking place around it.

This volume is a most worthy companion to the other classics of the Culver canon, General Gignilliat's "Arms and the Boy" and Robert B.D. Hartman's "Pass in Review." Together, they clearly set forth the lineaments of the Culver Way. This is necessary — and profoundly enjoyable — reading for all who love this extraordinary institution. Culver changes lives. It changed mine.

John Buxton's "Why Culver" will help you understand how it has done so for so many for so long; and why it will continue to do for generations to come.

Miles D. White
Chairman of the Board of
The Culver Educational Foundation

Why Culver

When and why does a relationship begin? There are always people and experiences that are obviously connected in some way to the start of a relationship — a formal meeting, a conversation on the phone, a chance meeting, or an introduction. When it comes to one's relationship with Culver, however, there is never any confusion about the steps that led to that person's connection to Culver.

After Pam and I had accepted the offer to come to Culver, then Chairman of the Board of Trustees, James A. Henderson, suggested we get out and meet the alumni base. The vehicle for getting us together with "our" alumni, was luncheon meetings in cities across the country. We would invite a dozen or so prominent alumni in a city to lunch for a "meet and greet." This served two important purposes: (1) Provide the opportunity for us to hear about our new school from those who knew Culver well; and (2) Remind those alumni, as they heard their own Culver relationship stories, why Culver was so important to them. It also gave our alumni a peek behind the curtain in meeting and hearing our story about how we began our relationship with this storied but sometimes misunderstood institution — one often referred to as "the best school most people have not heard of…or…the best kept secret in America."

The order of presentation was always the same. Jim Henderson, who seemed to know everyone's stories before we began, because he had been thoroughly involved with Culver since his graduation in 1952, and since he was the son of the Dean of Admissions who had admitted most of the men in the groups, introduced us and then asked each individual to tell us how each had learned about and ultimately arrived at Culver. He was asking them how what had become a lifelong relationship for them had started.

I had known from my days as an English teacher that there are only seven major themes or archetypes from which all stories originate. There are five similarly visible themes in the stories of these Culver graduates:

The first and most obvious connection was that many were carrying on his or her parents' or grandparents' traditions. Culver was a family school, and it was not unusual to have intergenerational traditions in which newer members of the same family followed those who had preceded them — fathers, mothers, uncles, brothers, sisters, and cousins.

The second theme was as school age children they had been introduced by their fathers or friends of their fathers to Culver, because it would give them a better chance of surviving the international conflicts looming on the horizon — World War II, Korea and Vietnam. Many of these men were members of the "Greatest Generation" and their families understood that Culver training might be advantageous. Through

A battalion parade with the earliest location of Woodcraft Camp tents visible in the background, circa 1920.

Boy Scouts of America co-founder Dan Beard was the founding director of Culver's Woodcraft Camp, serving for four years starting in 1912. Here he is pictured with campers in front of the original Riding Hall.

the Class of 1942, because of Culver's status as a Senior ROTC (Reserve Officers Training Corps) unit, Culver graduates were commissioned Second Lieutenants in the U.S. Army. Even after that policy changed during World War II, Culver's reputation and training afforded many of them a fast track to Officers' Candidate School in the various branches of service or advanced placement in ROTC programs in colleges and universities.

In 1946, Culver was designated a junior (JROTC) unit by the Army and maintained that affiliation until 1988.

The third explanation was that community leaders and educators from their cities or towns had suggested to their families that Culver would give their children "the best foundation for the future," because it provided excellence in academics and personal growth and development.

The Summer School provided the fourth explanation.

Every summer, Culver attracts over 1,350 boys and girls to its unique summer programs. Typically students come from 45 states and 25 countries. A third of them come from overseas. Half are of high school age in what Culver calls the Upper Schools. Half are in a younger age group from 9 to 14, which we call the Woodcraft Camp. Both age groups are focused on student leadership, responsibility, and achievement. They gain confidence, new skills and interests, and have fun, in just six short weeks.

For many, their experience at Culver's legendary Summer Naval School and Woodcraft Camp convinced them that the approach they were experiencing as Summer Midshipmen, members of the Summer School of Horsemanship Squadron, or as Beavers or Cubs in the Woodcraft Camp suited them well and would serve them just as well in the "Winter School."

The fifth reason was a process starting with an ad in the back of Boys' Life Magazine. As Culver was gaining in prominence for all the reasons above, it determined that advertising was a good way to extend its reach nationally, so ads placed in national magazines or newspapers gave Culver that exposure. And Boys' Life was extremely popular with boys who were embracing the narratives of the military and "manliness" (godliness) in general. Culver offered its own brand of military training and had done so right after its beginning in 1894. For a brief period, Culver also advertised effectively in the National Geographic magazine.

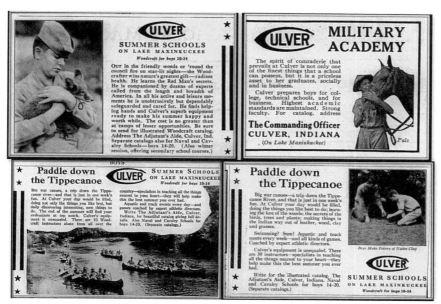

Advertisements for both Culver Summer Schools and Camps and Culver Military Academy, featuring the distinctive Culver logo.

There were certainly other explanations, like its national reputation for outstanding academics, that had landed it prominent coverage in Life magazine, Look magazine, Time magazine and The Saturday Evening Post in the early 1960s; or that from the 1930s through the 1960s Culver's college placement destination list included all the most competitive colleges and universities in the country.

Many of the graduates we met talked about showing up at Culver for the Admissions process and taking the test, only to find that their straight A records at home obviously didn't mean much. A great percentage of them were told that as well as they believed they had done at home, "this was Culver, and the standards are different.

But we will give you a chance to prove your worth as a Summer School student to see if you have what it takes." So many of these highly successful businessmen and titans of industry from all over the United States and Mexico had been willing to do what it took to be admitted and spent a summer at Culver to prove they could manage the Winter School program. In addition to giving the boys an opportunity to further their academic training against the backdrop of a rigorous physical summer, this approach also spoke to Culver's remarkable attention to detail for each boy's progress. Until the 1950s, each boy had his height, weight, and posture benchmarked annually.

As a former Director of Admissions at a highly selective boarding school in New England, I was surprised to hear that any of these graduates would have needed "an extra year…or even a summer of extra study." Then it occurred to me that Jim Henderson had mentioned that his father, Col. John Henderson, was Director of Admissions and was responsible for filling both the summer and winter schools. This approach to setting the hook and adding to the summer numbers was both a brilliant sales tool and a successful admissions strategy. When I mentioned this to Jim, he was more than surprised — he was in denial. But the more he considered the possibilities, the more he acknowledged them. He saw this as an example of leadership in action and an indication that his father was assuring that those who matriculated valued the opportunity and embraced the challenge: a good Culver response, as we would come to understand.

Col. John Henderson was not the only member of the Henderson family who had legendary sales skills. By setting up these meetings, Jim was not only educating Pam and me about Culver and its special history, but he was also introducing us to as impressive yet humble a group as anyone could imagine. We were learning about both the quality of the graduates and about their deep respect for, and commitment to, their school. Their pride in the "Academy" became our pride for them and, by extension, for their school.

The conversations during these luncheons also provided me with both the opportunity to familiarize myself with the stories of Culver and a chance to explain how Pam and I happened to be sitting here among them. We had been in the "head of schools' seat," as it were, for a few months, so we already had our own impressions to share and experiences to relate. Most important was the story of how our relationship with Culver had started and why we were there now.

At first blush, I thought that our Culver story had begun when we received a call from a search agency in the Midwest, asking me if I would be interested in applying for the position of the President of the Culver Academies in Culver, Indiana. The caller explained rather quickly that Culver was a military school in Indiana and that the school was looking for a new chief executive. I responded quickly that I did not believe I had the background needed to run a military school, but that I knew a lieutenant colonel who would be a perfect candidate, if they were interested. I assumed the issue of Culver was now settled. How wrong I was.

A few weeks later, I received another call from an architect I had worked with on a major building project at our former school some years before. I had not heard from her in years, so receiving a call from her in Sweden was surprising. I returned the call immediately and after a quick catching up, she delivered her message/advice:

"John, I thought about you and Pam recently when I was visiting a wonderful and impressive school in Indiana. It is called the Culver Academies, and it is looking for new leadership, since its longtime President, who was formerly the Dean at Dartmouth College, is retiring. I really think you should look at it. You guys would be great there."

I was pleased our friends and former colleagues were thinking about us, but I was more interested in the coincidence of receiving phone calls twice in two weeks about a school I could not remember ever having heard of. I told Pam about it, and her only question was,

"So how is Jonella doing?"

"Great, she's back in Sweden, but she was working on a Graham Gund project at Culver and thought we should look carefully at the opening for their Head of Schools position."

About a week later the phone rang again, and Lance Odden was on the line. While I knew of him as the Headmaster of the Taft School and the "Dean of Boarding School Headmasters," I was not a friend or even an acquaintance of his. Getting a call from him was something of an event. We chatted briefly, and he moved right to his message:

"John, there is an excellent school in Indiana that needs a new headmaster. They need a wrestler at the helm, so I think you'd be perfect for the job."

Pam and I were talking later in the day and I mentioned that Lance Odden had called.

"Who's he?" she asked.

"He is the Headmaster at Taft and he was calling to let me know about the opening at Culver. He thinks I should apply."

"What did he say?"

"Not much. He said it was an excellent school and that it needed a wrestler to run it."

"That's odd. Wait a minute, isn't that the school Jonella called about? This can't be a coincidence."

We agreed that there was at least a minor conspiracy going on here or some significant coincidences. And then the next piece of the puzzle appeared. Pam and I were seated at dinner during a meeting for an Independent School Insurance Board of Directors, and one of our dinner partners was the Chief Business Officer of Culver. He introduced himself, explained that Culver, like our school, had been one of the founding members of this new insurance company, and that he wanted to encourage us to look carefully at the leadership opening at Culver. He was a former East Coast private school administrator, and he wanted to be certain we understood that quality education does not end at the Hudson River.

Pam and I were now on the case, formally. What was Culver? Why did people think Culver was such a good match for us? Who or what was the connection among all these people and this well-kept secret of a school? We didn't have to wait long to get answers to these questions. The phone rang again the following week, and this time the caller identified himself as the Chairman of the Board of Trustees of Culver. His name was Jim Henderson, and he explained that he had been talking with a northeastern search consultant, who happened to be a friend of mine, and asked for a few names for the Culver search. The consultant had suggested he talk to the Buxtons.

Jim then explained that he understood I was on sabbatical and taking courses at Boston University, so I was in Boston regularly. He, too, came to Boston to speak at the Harvard Business School from time to time and asked if we could meet to talk. He was professional, articulate, serious, and extremely welcoming and flexible. He apologized for not having more dates to offer for our meeting, but he assured me that if the dates proposed did not line up well with my schedule, he would make a special trip for the meeting. Having this meeting was clearly important to him.

As you can imagine, I was eager to learn why a school that could and would marshal such impressive resources to find appropriate leadership for the future, was not a household name. Maybe this meeting would be the first step in answering that important question. I agreed to meet him in Boston the following week. The rest, as they say, is history…the history of our relationship with a remarkable school.

Chapter One: The Proof is in the Pudding

This meeting with the Chairman of the Board of Culver was scheduled to take place at a hotel in Boston. I was on sabbatical from the school I had served for 29 years, where I had been a teacher, junior administrator for off-campus learning, the Director of College Advising, the Director of Admissions, and, most recently, the administrator responsible for finance and operations. I also had been a teacher and a coach for 29 years. My sabbatical was long overdue — usually sabbaticals are offered after 7–10 years of experience — but the timing was perfect. We had decided that it made sense to complete our service to the only school we had ever worked for, and that regardless of how the year away went, we would not be returning. This was going to be a terminal sabbatical. It was time for a change.

We were excited to undertake one more adventure in our lives before retirement, and we wanted a year to determine whether that adventure would be in education or business. Literally, we walked into the year of study with a totally clean slate and open minds. I began to search for the perfect opportunity for study and reflection, and I found one at Boston University to design my own PhD program in education and management. The university had both a School of Education and a School of Management. My task was to couple the right courses together to create a cogent program of study that would prepare me to think more deeply and creatively about the two areas of work I knew the most about. The decision to do this may actually have been the beginning of our relationship with Culver.

I spent the week before my meeting with Jim Henderson studying for and writing about school and business leadership. Fortunately for me, in my Leadership courses in the School of Management, I had been tasked to write a letter to send to myself a year into the future, discussing what I would be doing then. I thought this exercise was something teachers assigned their students in high schools to remind them to think about the future and to plan accordingly. With a bit of skepticism, I launched into the assignment. I was surprised how quickly I determined the best path for the future. As I wrote about what I planned to do next, I was reminded how important casual mentors had been in my career. I thought about all those teachers and administrators who helped guide me early in my career as an educator. I recalled vividly the advice given to me by seasoned professionals as I took on a variety of new leadership roles that I had had little experience with before taking on the new responsibilities. I had been the beneficiary of three decades of customized good advice, and I was now in the same position as my mentors to support and guide the careers of those entering the field of education. Maybe I had a responsibility to continue the tradition of mentoring teachers and administrators, using and sharing the knowledge and experience I had been fortunate to have been given. That was what my own reflections were telling me. By the time I walked into the hotel for the meeting, I was clear that running a school was in my future. Now I had to figure out whether this surprising place — Culver — was going to play a part in our adventure.

Jim was waiting for me when I arrived, but that should not have been surprising to anyone who understands Culver or who knows Jim Henderson. As Easterners, we were used to people arriving late because of traffic, meetings running over, and last minute phone calls. But that is not the Culver way. Punctuality is a form of respect

and an obligation for serious people. Lateness suggests that you believe for some reason that your time is more valuable or important than that of the person you are meeting. Of course, Jim Henderson was prompt.

My first impression of him was positive: warm, welcoming, bright-eyed, and professionally engaged. He reminded me of Jimmy Stewart playing a CEO. Jim was relaxed but it was clear why this meeting was such a priority for him. He was looking for the next leader for Culver, and he wanted to get it right. I was reminded of the saying that "You don't send a boy to do a man's job." This search process was his responsibility, and because it was a Culver search, it was deeply personal for him. Regardless of, and possibly because of my history as an experienced board-

Chairman of the Board, Jim Henderson WC '47 CMA '52 and Head of Schools, John Buxton, honor Culver graduate and Trustee Emeritus, George M. Steinbrenner WC '44 '48.

ing school administrator and school person, if I did not measure up to the key characteristics they were looking for, this process would go no further.

I have no idea how long the meeting lasted, but I do recall phoning Pam immediately after the meeting and telling her I had just met the most remarkable person and that we would be visiting this mysterious place called Culver. Pam asked whether Jim had had a specific agenda, and I replied that he seemed interested in two things: how much of a "preppie" I was, and whether I believed in student leadership. I explained that he had no interest in bringing in an eastern boarding school person to make Culver more like Exeter or Andover. Culver had its own differentiated brand of excellence, just as those schools did, and Culver would always be Culver. Primarily, that meant having a commitment to student leadership.

I spent a significant amount of time reflecting on my conversation with Jim, and the more I analyzed the conversation, the more intrigued I became. He was not drawing the student leadership and character line in the sand because he did not care about academics. He had attended Princeton upon his graduation from Culver, served in the U.S. Navy, and graduated from Harvard Business School. He also was chairing the Princeton University Board of Trustees at the time of the Culver search. Academics mattered to Jim, but not at the expense of Culver's commitment to leadership, accountability, and personal responsibility. We would soon learn that these were feelings strongly held by many members of the Culver Board and alumni. They were not interested in a person who wanted to envision a different Culver. Rather, they were looking to partner with a new school leader who would ensure an even better version of this important school.

My reflections about the search process also helped me recall two prior interactions with Culver, reflections that reminded me that the first call from the search consultant had not been my first experience with Culver. Our son had interviewed with the Dean of the Academies at Culver when he was looking for an internship opportunity after his graduation from college nearly 8 years earlier. Our son had called to say he had met an extremely impressive individual representing Culver, a man who directed their successful teaching intern program. He explained to us that the person's description of this remarkable school had been so compelling that if Culver had been located closer to the East Coast, he would have jumped at the opportunity. He was truly impressed and interested.

We also had had an even earlier experience with Culver involving one of our favorite students at our former school. It had occurred in the early 1980s, nearly 20 years before we discovered Culver. I was the Director of Admissions at that time, and this young man from the border of Southern California had come to interview for a place in our tenth grade class. The challenge was that spaces available for new tenth graders were scarce. We would be admitting only 25 boys from a pool of nearly 200, so the successful candidate had to have everything going for him. This young man did not fit the stereotype of the successful 10th grade male applicant for our school. He would be transferring in from a military school in the Midwest, not coming to us from a traditional "feeder school." He did not have that singular and proven talent that most successful tenth grade applicants possessed. And, the most challenging negative of all, he wanted to transfer because he was looking for a place that would help him gain acceptance to the college of his choice — Stanford. He had relatively modest testing, but his grades were good, and he had an honesty and a character that shone through brilliantly during the interview.

Most important, his story fascinated me. He had grown up in this border town between California and Mexico where his family ran a large and successful alfalfa farm. His father, who did not accompany him on the visit "because he was running the farm," was a self-made man, and his mother was a force of nature. It was clear, however, that the transfer idea was his. He carried the conversation. In short, he explained in simple and direct terms, but not emotional terms, that he was attending a great school, but some of its practices were making it difficult for him to realize his dream of attending Stanford. I asked him to elucidate.

His explanation fascinated me. "I go to a military school and when you get into trouble — which is easy to do there because they have so many rules — they make you march." I pressed him for further details. "You report to an office where the O.C. (Officer in Charge) directs you to proceed to a triangle of ground outside the barracks, and there you march for a specific amount of time, reflecting on what you had done to warrant the disciplinary response."

He went on to explain that he understood the disincentive concept, but because it was hard for him not to get into trouble because of his study schedule, he felt there was no getting around this problem. So, he decided he needed to transfer schools.

"Why this school?" I queried.

"Because you get more graduating seniors into Stanford than my school does."

"And you know this, how?"

"My brother applied to Stanford last year and didn't get in, and no one from his class was accepted either."

"Where is your brother going to college?"

"Vanderbilt."

"But that is a terrific and highly competitive school."

"But I want to go to Stanford, and your school had five students accepted there last year."

Here was an eager, honest, principled, ambitious, unaffected young man sitting in front of me, asking me whether I would support his application to Stanford three years hence if he did all that was required of him and excelled academically, athletically, and personally. This was a compelling offer and certainly unlike any I had encountered before. I took his file to Committee, and everyone agreed that this young man needed to be admitted. The school he was coming from: Culver. "What's Culver?" someone on the Committee had asked.

Now you might imagine that his thought process about needing to get away from Culver cast a negative shadow on the school. I never saw it as such. He was a pragmatist. He understood that Culver's practices and policies were instituted because they had a mission and a system that made it necessary for everyone to follow the same guidelines. Culver was not a "create your own adventure" kind of place. At Culver, you did Culver, and you followed Culver's guidelines. If you decided to stay up later than the "lights out" curfew, you marched. If you were late to practice because you were studying for a big test, you marched. You were not more important than your peers simply because you thought you had a good reason for not adhering to the rules. There actually was no good reason. You would be held accountable. He understood this, respected it, and, therefore, had to prioritize his decisions; and as a somewhat new participant in the Eastern boarding school game, he was now taking personal responsibility for his actions and pressing on toward his goal. His profile was totally refreshing to the members of a faculty committee used to seeing much more carefully crafted justifications or more of a traditional, cookie cutter narrative.

For whatever reason, whenever I thought of him, I thought of the wonderful young man who came into our school as a Fourth Former (10th grade) and not as "the kid from Culver." This is probably because he went on to achieve highest honors in the classroom with a more than challenging course load, to captain teams, and to comport himself as a leader and a young man of character for three years. He also applied Early Decision to Stanford, and despite his mediocre testing, he was admitted.

Just as interesting, his college essay on driving a combine throughout the night as part of his farm responsibilities was chosen as one of the ten best admission application essays submitted the year he applied. I would have been hard pressed to even recall that his school had been Culver, but his school, as it turned out, was Culver…and as we would come to appreciate, what made us love him in the admissions process and as a student, and later as a friend of ours, were all those qualities that we now associate with Culver.

We were beginning to see a pattern forming. We had met only two truly remarkable Culver people, and each impressed us as people with whom we would be more than pleased to associate. Added to that, one of our best proxies, our son, had nearly made the decision to travel to Indiana for an internship when he had excellent offers from well-known and respected Eastern boarding schools in hand because of the approach of a Culver Dean who believed that Culver would be a perfect place for our son to begin his career. He must have seen in our son what we would come to see in Culver. That, too, would have been a perfect match.

We had to deal with the present, however, and we had been contacted by several schools about leadership opportunities at their schools. Also, time was getting short. We were in the late fall of the year, and most of the schools we were talking to wanted to announce their choice of a new head of school by the first of the year. This meant we were on a fast-track schedule, and we wanted to be certain we had time to educate ourselves fully about Culver, which was moving from longshot to favorite quickly.

Pam and I boarded the plane in Boston and flew to O'Hare, where we were met by the Director of Alumni Affairs. He was exceedingly pleasant, articulate, and ironically, a devotee of the man who had interviewed our son, as well as a former intern himself. He drove us through the night for about 100 miles southeast of Chicago, and by the time we had reached this sleepy little town of 1700 people, all we had seen were railroad tracks, darkened fields, and sharp "S" turns to navigate the cornfields. He did include a stop at a famous restaurant on the highway that featured every turkey dish imaginable, a little local color, and some much-needed sustenance.

We arrived at a beautiful and well-positioned guest house right on the Academy's main road — Academy Road, which bisected the school's grounds. We were told to set our alarms, so we would be prepared for a 7:00 am pickup for breakfast to begin a day during which we would be "flies on the wall," as we acclimated ourselves to the Academy. At 7 am sharp (that punctuality thing again) the doorbell rang, and our first appointment stood waiting on the front porch, outlined by the most beautiful background imaginable. Directly across the street was a campus of lovely and traditional brick and limestone buildings skillfully placed on the banks of the majestic, spring-fed Lake Maxinkuckee — 2,000 acres, 10 miles around, and nearly 100 feet deep. Our guide introduced herself as the Head of the (Unified) Arts Department and a member and co-chair of the Campus Advisory Council — the faculty-staff arm of the search process. She couldn't have been more welcoming or helpful.

We proceeded to walk down Academy Road to a dining hall purportedly boasting the largest unsupported ceiling in the United States. The Dining or Mess Hall, as it was referred to, included seating for over 1,000. It was huge and magnificent, replete with beautiful mosaics depicting Native American life in the late 19th century in north central Indiana. There were four serving lines, and we took our place at the end of one. Immediately, we were offered a place in the front of the line by several students, but understanding school dining services and imagining how pressed the students' schedules were, we politely declined their kind offers and waited our turns — pleasantly surprised that a group of hungry 14–18 year olds were polite enough or well informed enough to have been so courteous.

Culver's stately Dining Hall, built in 1910, serves thousands daily.

During breakfast we were given the itinerary for the visit. There was not much "fly on the wall" time included. We were scheduled to meet individually with nearly every member of the Administration and almost all members of the Campus Advisory Committee, which was comprised to ensure faculty and staff input to the Search Committee. We were also invited to watch some practices and rehearsals. Then, as we prepared ourselves for our departure, we were scheduled to have a final meeting with Jim Henderson, so he could answer any questions we had about what we had seen during the day. As one would expect, we had many — so many that he invited us to spend the night to continue the give and take conversation later into the day and allow us to attend a basketball game that night. Then, in what we were learning was true Culver fashion, he assured us he would fly us back in time to attend an event we were scheduled for that next evening. We agreed.

Once back in New Hampshire, we faced the first in a series of important decisions: first, we had to unpack the visit and determine whether we were serious about considering a move to the Midwest. Then, if we were determined to respond affirmatively to an offer to become a finalist in the Culver process, how could we manage the timing of the Culver process with that of the other school we were being asked to consider? Finally, if we said "yes" to Culver's expression of interest, would we remove our names from consideration at any other school? And we had only a few days to make this monumental decision.

However, there would still need to be two intermediary steps before the Culver search committees could decide whether we merited finalist status. It began with the Trustee Search Committee's visit to our school to get the "ground truth" about the Buxtons, and, following that visit, as serious an approach to background checking as you could imagine. I recall Jim Henderson explaining Culver's background checking process by asking first for permission to call our references. I assured him he could contact anyone on the list. He pressed on: "Would it be acceptable to ask each of those contacted as a reference if he or she knew anyone else to whom they could also speak?" "Certainly," I responded. Then he asked whether we would be open to have a private investigator investigate our backgrounds to "check us out" further? "That would not be a problem for us. Please do any and everything you feel is necessary to give you the confidence you need to have to proceed with the process," we responded.

Then there was a final step in the screening process:

"Leaders from the Board of Trustees would appreciate having the opportunity to meet you in Concord and, if possible and appropriate, the group would be coming in two groups," Jim Henderson explained.

"Please, encourage them to do so; we would love to meet them."

A few days later, enough private jets arrived in our tiny Concord airport to convince the airport officials there must have been an unannounced visit by a candidate for the upcoming Presidential election. But it was the members of the Culver Board making time to do their due diligence. On the first visit we greeted the CEO of Landmark Communications (The Weather Channel), the CEO of Rohm and Haas, and the CEO of Crown Equipment Corporation. "Are these all graduates of Culver?" I asked Jim Henderson, who was also in attendance. "Absolutely," he responded.

On the second visit a day or two later, we welcomed Jim Henderson, the CEO of Cummins Engine Company, a prominent physician from Michigan, and the CEO of the Tribune Company, owner of the Chicago Cubs, my second favorite team. (Pam and I are die-hard Red Sox fans, but we have a new-found, Culver-based respect for the Yankees!)

If these people were representative of the quality of Culver graduates, this must have been a special place when they graduated. Here were public and private sector leaders taking personal time from what must have been incredibly complicated and busy schedules to serve their high school and to help ensure that each of them had the chance to meet and evaluate the people being considered as their next head of schools. They were also making the point that this was their school and it mattered to them.

As it turned out, we were invited to be a finalist in the process and return to Culver for final interviews.

Fast forward a few weeks, and we were traveling back to Culver into the teeth of a serious winter storm to keep the search process on schedule. This trip was for a series of formal interviews with administrators, faculty, and students. The visit would be equally busy, with every appointment scheduled end on end. We joked that they must have been interested in testing our levels of stamina.

Pam and I spent part of the day together, meeting important members of the leadership team and some additional Trustees, as well as having some important time with the students to gather and assess their points of view. The Search Committee had also done its homework on Pam and her interests and had scheduled a visit for her to the local hospital, knowing that Pam had been both a volunteer and then hired as the coordinator for the pulmonary rehabilitation program in the hospital in our current city. The process was thoughtfully arranged and incredibly helpful. We ended the day with a meet and greet with the community of teachers, administrators, and hourly workers, after which they provided us with a few hours to put our heads together, reflect on our time there and gauge where we were in the process. We were scheduled to have dinner that evening with the grandson of the fourth "Superintendent" of the Academies — General Leigh Gignilliat — who was arguably one of the seminal leaders in the Culver story. This Trustee and his wife were a final gate, as it were, in the process. For them, especially, Culver was deeply personal, so the choice of the next head of school was a decision of huge significance to them.

As we discovered, winter on the Culver campus has a beauty all its own.

We went to a small local restaurant, Papa's, and had as pleasant and engaging an evening as we could ever recall. We shared stories, educational priorities, and life philosophy and values. They were simply the next in a series of Culver people who were impressive in so many ways: down-to-earth, humble, and generous with their time. More importantly, they cared deeply about their Academy. In fact, they had met and had their first dates at Culver.

We spent the next day trudging through the snow around this beautiful 1800-acre campus, meeting those we had not met the day before, having lunch with students, watching practices, and preparing for a dinner with most members of the Board, who had also flown in during this snow storm — in 12 inches of new snow. Jim Henderson had asked if he could drive us to his home where the dinner would take place, and he hoped it would be agreeable if he came a few minutes early to discuss the process going forward. His approach throughout the entire process had been respectful, professional, and wonderfully genuine. He was for us the embodiment of Culver's values and virtues that we had been experiencing with all others associated with Culver's leadership. We had been so impressed that Pam and I decided that if we were chosen to lead this Academy, we would make a game of trying to find in our travels just one Culver graduate we thought did not meet the standards of Culver's Code of Conduct, i.e. didn't act like a good Culver man or woman should. And we knew it would be a challenging search.

Our trip back to New Hampshire the next morning in the ice and snow would have been harrowing if we had had any free time to contemplate the dangers of flying through a blizzard or landing on a sheet of ice at the airport in Manchester. We had no time for that. We were making our decision about whether our last great adventure in education was going to play out in the middle of the country at America's "best kept secret" or on the East Coast at a lesser version of the professionalism, quality of mission, and high level of engagement of the students we had experienced during our visits to Culver.

Our return flight discussion was focused and intense. However, it could be distilled down to four basic yet critical issues: (1) This would be a decision between staying close to our family, who would be living only a few hours away, or moving to the middle of the country — a full day's drive and at least 5 hours (travel to the airport to arrival at our children's homes) by air. (2) This was a question of which head of school position provided the best opportunity because of its challenges and needs and the skill set we possessed to address them. (3) This was a question of which Board of Trustees seemed to be more likely to challenge us to be our best and to work with us in a true partnership. (4) Finally, this was a question of whether we were the best people to lead a school with a military background and military programs, in both summer and winter, into a future with understanding and respect.

If we had known then what we knew only a few short months later, we could have given the "if asked to serve, we would be honored to do so" response immediately. Regardless, by the time we slid across the icy landing strip at the airfield and were greeted by a close friend who had braved the weather to pick us up, we knew we would be starting a relationship with a new school and a wonderful new group of people, in the Midwest…if selected.

Now, it was time to get started on educating ourselves about Culver, in earnest.

Chapter Two: Preparation, Preparation, Preparation

Since we were on sabbatical and I was in the position to determine the topic for my dissertation as part of my course of study, I had the time and the options that were not usually available to most new heads of school and therefore could study Culver. I immediately contacted my dissertation professor to discuss the idea, and he was both encouraging and curious. He reminded me that writing a history of a school would not pass muster for this research, but that if I could come up with a research topic that had validity, he would be very interested, especially since I would have the opportunity for "action research" while working there. In the paper I would be proposing solutions to real challenges that the Academy faced, and these could be evaluated in real time. This was a win-win.

I began with the past. I have always believed that before you determine where you are going, you need to understand where you have been. I contacted Culver and asked them to send me all the material they had on the history of The Academy. I was amazed. I had been working in a well-known and well-regarded boarding school for 30 years and rarely had I heard any narratives of the School that served as points of pride or examples of right action on the part of the School that symbolized its values or helped define its Mission. Yet, Culver was blessed with dozens of them. This was yet another opportunity for a true relationship to begin.

I began by reading a copy of the book that the trustee we had had dinner with at Papa's, who was the grandson of the fourth Superintendent of the Academy, had given us as a gift. Arms and the Boy was written by then Superintendent, General Leigh Gignilliat, in early 1916; it described the model for a school — in this case Culver — which would use the principles advanced by the Greeks (Plato and Aristotle) and the lessons learned from the Civil War to create an educational environment that would address the intellectual, academic, social, physical, and emotional development and leadership of its students. Woven into its pages were examples of what

Leigh Gignilliat's Arms and the Boy, published in 1916, explained the educational underpinnings and outcomes of the Military School approach.

Left: Gen. Leigh R. Gignilliat on horseback, circa 1930s, oversees the horse-drawn artillery during a garrison parade, with Culver's riding hall and armory in the background.

would become the essence of Culver: the development of a boy's character through his engagement with specific habits of mind and heart, as well as training in specific tasks, which would help give him confidence and a sense of personal responsibility and accountability.

Gignilliat was trained at Virginia Military Institute (VMI) and believed in the practices and principles of military training. He believed that good citizenship could best be taught by the principles used to train leaders in the military. Learning to take care of oneself and then learning to be responsible and accountable for the uniform, bunk, and requirements were the first two building blocks of learning to be a leader. If these requirements were met, they were followed by learning to take care of and accept responsibility for others. The final level of training was preparation to take responsibility for and leadership of the program and those leading and directing their soldiers. The calculus was that the country needed both good leaders and good followers, and the U.S. military had developed the best model to ensure that we had these characteristics to support the Republic and the "common weal." This is how VMI trained him. He understood that taking responsibility for others and doing the right thing, always, were credos in which he believed deeply.

Colonel Alexander Fleet (right), a distinguished educator and classical scholar who served Culver as Superintendent from 1896 to 1910, and Lt. Leigh Gignilliat, who served as his Commandant from 1897 to 1910, and then as Superintendent from 1910 to 1939.

Gignilliat's approach was additionally galvanized by two important experiences: his classical education and his experiences not only as a soldier but also as an officer. As a student of Plato and Aristotle, he would have learned about the importance of developing the model of the citizen soldier for his democracy. From Aristotle he learned that "we are what we repeatedly do." It is also probable that he was conversant with the speech delivered in the early 1900s by the educational philosopher from Harvard University, William James, entitled "The Moral Equivalent of War." Somewhat ironic is the fact that William James was a pacifist, but he understood that our society needed certain virtues that unfortunately, but conclusively, could only be honed in the context of war. He presented his utopian vision of a country that would create important and practical ways for its young men to learn the ideals associated with militarism.

James wrote the following:

> "Militarism is the great preserver of our ideals of hardihood, and human life with no use for hardihood would be contemptible. Without risks or prizes for the darer, history would be insipid indeed; and there is a type of military character which everyone feels that the races should never cease to breed, for everyone is sensitive to its superiority. The duty is incumbent on mankind, of keeping military character in stock — if keeping them, if not for use, then as ends in themselves and as pure as perfection — so that Roosevelt's weaklings and mollycoddles may not end by making everything else disappear from the face of nature."

He then quoted H.G. Wells, legendary author of "The Time Machine" and "War of the Worlds," to make his point more strongly. Wells, he wrote, said that he believed that:

> "...the conceptions of order and discipline, the tradition of service and devotion, of physical fitness, unstinted exertion, and universal responsibility, which universal military duty is now teaching, will remain a permanent acquisition when the last ammunition has been used in the fireworks that celebrate the final peace."

James stated that he believed, as Wells did, that it would be simply preposterous if the only force that could work the ideals of honor and standards of efficiency into English or American natures should be the fear of being killed. He made the additional claim that our national education system could and should provide this training. Education would be the moral equivalent of war.

Gignilliat understood from his personal education and his significant military experiences that there were important lessons and perspectives a young person would derive from a carefully constructed program of military education. He believed that those who had served in the military had learned to embrace responsibility, had learned what it meant to be fully accountable, and understood that citizens in this country needed to have developed the traits of character if they were to serve and lead their country — in times of war and peace.

Gignilliat had taken over the reins at Culver from an experienced military veteran, Col. Alexander Fleet, and together Fleet and he crafted this special Culver Military school model, which was what you might expect from two citizen soldiers. They both valued academic excellence and personal excellence; and they believed young men who were exposed to a system that required the exercise of regular duties and responsibilities would form the habits that would serve them well in life. They believed America's youth needed to learn self-discipline in a system that stressed the concepts of teamwork and personal integrity. Years later Jim Henderson described a particularly successful cadet as having "the look of eagles." He was capturing in a simple phrase what Lee, James, Wells, and both Fleet and Gignilliat were describing as the outcome of an educational process that resulted in "hardihood" and the military education of character.

They also understood that boys learned better by doing. John Dewey, the well-respected educational philosopher, was convinced that the learning process was more effective if it included practice as well as theory. His concept was gaining popularity nationwide in the early 20th century, and the activities of the military provided a nearly perfect model to assist young men in the challenges of navigating their youth and their teenage years. Now, Gignilliat needed evidence that his system was working as advertised.

While I read this text, I was reminded of my youth. I had spent countless Saturday mornings getting up at the crack of dawn and exiting the house to meet several neighborhood friends to "play soldier." We were officially members of the Union Army, and while I have no memory of the enemy, we did drills; we crawled over muddy terrain, hills and dales; and we fought our hearts out. I don't recall any metrics we might have

Bob Hartman served the Academy in a number of roles including history teacher, Admissions Director, and Alumni Director from 1958 to 1994. After retirement, he returned to Culver from 2000 to 2012 as School Historian, writing a number of books and articles on Culver's history.

BOOTS AND SADDLES

Bugle Calls to a Century of the Black Horse Troop
1897-1997

Pass in Review was Bob Hartman's first effort to capture the spirit and history of the Academy in book form.

PASS IN REVIEW

CULVER: A Century in the Making

used to determine our success, but we would spend the entire day in the pursuit of victory with honor. My question was, therefore, "How would this work in the 21st century?"

Next, I read a copy of a history of Culver written by one of the Academy's long-serving faculty members, Robert B.D. Hartman. He was a history teacher and loved Culver. He was also thoroughly convinced from his research that the most influential person in the long history of Culver up to that point was General Leigh Gignilliat, who had both created and seized upon opportunities to bring Culver into the national conversation about great schools, had set the model in granite, and had not only espoused but also demonstrated that the system worked. Hartman's history, entitled Pass in Review, chronicled the stories and important narratives of the Academy Bob loved. He described a school that had boasted a legendary faculty, a legendary past, and proud traditions as the best of all military schools. But his history concluded with the arrival of coeducation in the early 1970s. We were now almost three decades from those halcyon days, but it was clear this school had had quite a successful run.

Bob also authored other historical pieces on Culver, including, Boots and Saddles, the History of Culver's Black Horse Troop, and The Grand Parade, Bob's homage to Culver's past through the publication of a collection of interesting and significant vignettes. Each painted a picture of a grand Academy with a storied past, a talented, successful, and devoted alumni body, and a history of service and leadership.

All this was reassuring to Pam and me, but there was more to the story, as Paul Harvey was fond of saying. The materials the Academy had sent also included reports shared recently with the Board of Trustees that expressed some concern about the challenges faced by military schools in the modern era. Admissions, while perfectly adequate, was showing signs of weakening; and the analysis was that the military system was the reason.

Competitive and popular prep schools around the country were mostly modeled on the British system of schools like Eton and Harrow, where the students were accepted because of their natural gifts or family backgrounds and given enough freedom and support to blossom individually. The military school model, on the other hand, was truly an American approach, more behavioral in nature. The American philosophy did not simply rely on a positive environment, which ensured proper sunlight and watering, created by caring and somewhat attentive teachers. Students in the American system were modeled on the U.S. Military Academies like West Point and the Naval Academy at Annapolis, which had a required academic and personal growth curriculum and were intentional about teaching the skills and habits of service and leadership. American schools did not leave as much to chance, and while this American model may

Cadets in formation on the parade field, early 1900s.

have suited young people in the 20th century, it did not seem to be wearing as well with modern youth. The discipline, as well as the personal and physical requirements of the military environment, were time-consuming and did not have obvious appeal when weighed against a young person's ability to guide or educate him or herself.

Clearly, relevance was an issue. Also, the brand of all military boarding schools seemed to have taken a reputational hit. I then recalled listening to ads on the radio as I would drive to New York City for Board of Trustees' meetings for my former school — ads that suggested that a military academy in the area might be the perfect choice for you and your child, if he was experiencing problems at his current school or had lost his place in school due to behavioral issues. The "value proposition" of this military academy, it seemed, was to "send us your broken child and we will 'fix' him and return a responsible young man to you." It sounded very much like a "join the Marines and become a man," and I recall wondering how much business they had in their Admissions Office. I also wondered if there were other military academies and whether all were experiencing the same challenges.

That led me to a search of military academies in the U.S., and I learned that after the end of the Civil War, many military academies had sprung up around the country using this "American" approach to educating young citizens-to-be. Then as World War I approached and after its conclusion, the military academy model was embraced even more widely, and there were literally hundreds of schools nationally using this methodology and philosophy. After World War II and the Korean Conflict, the numbers had begun to decline, and as I was doing this research — in the late 1990s — there were only a few dozen military high schools still operating; and many of them were struggling financially due to shrinking "demand numbers" (candidates for admissions and college placement results).

Cadets slow marching to Culver's 2014 Veterans Day ceremony on Pershing Walk, so named for the visit of World War I Allied Commander Gen. John "Blackjack" Pershing to Culver in 1922.

I was not surprised to learn that there was a problem attracting students of the 1970s '80s and '90s to these schools. The most popular secondary school model after the social revolution of the 1960s offered nicer accommodations (dorms, as opposed to no-frills barracks), excellent academic programs, good athletic and Arts offerings, and more than acceptable college placement profiles. There was no marching, no parades, no room inspections, no responsibility for others, no leadership of and for others, and a modest commitment to service that was driven by the individual, not by the school.

Having spent 29 years at one of these exceedingly popular schools where the admissions ratio (those applying to those admitted) was in the neighborhood of 8–1, I could see the challenge. Remember the young man from California who felt that his biggest impediment to getting into Stanford was all the time he was spending on what seemed to him to be irrelevant activity — activity that was not improving him enough in a college's eyes to make him admissible? For the most competitive colleges, a student's scores, grades, extracurricular activities, and, fortunately or unfortunately, a student's background and/or connections determined whether he or she would be admitted. Student leadership was measured somewhat cynically, I believe, by determining whether or not the applicant had ever held an elected class office or served on the student council; and, more important, whether a student worked on a charity in his or her community. Students in general believed, therefore, that anything that interfered with this quest for the Holy Grail of acceptance to the competitive college of one's choice was a non-starter.

The challenge could also be stated in these terms: "As a student I want to be able to choose what my parents and I believe is in my best interest, and getting the scores, grades, and activities that will position me best for college admissions is the obvious approach. If there are time-consuming requirements at schools that are created to help me prepare myself for life — playing the long game, as it were — I am interested only to the extent that they excite and interest me." Or, students evaluated their choice of school, or even school type, as a zero-sum game: "If I do what I want, and I fail, then I understand it's my problem. If I do what you say I need to do, and I fail, it's my fault for listening to you and for attending your school." It's a win/lose proposition. Unfortunately, neither of these scenarios seemed to bode well for military schools at the turn of the 21st century.

Furthermore, as the positive memories and the favorable aura of the Great War and World War II became relics of the past, and in the face of the federal government's unfavorable management of the Vietnam War and the news reporting that surrounded it, soldiering and military activities were no longer the activities of choice for children on Saturday mornings. War has always been described as hell, but for the Greatest Generation and their fathers, it was never immoral. Now it was. Many of our great institutions were no longer trusted and were the most obvious target for the social revolution of the 1960s and beyond was our "Military Industrial Complex."

These were some of the reasons, I imagined as I did my research, that military schools were at risk as we entered the year 2000. They were being seen as antiquated models of what had once been part of the proud tradition of "American" education. Furthermore, they were more than likely struggling against the tide of financial equilibrium that beset all private schools in the 1970s. Single sex schools (all male and all girls' schools) faced a Hobbesian choice: Move away from their historical commitment to single sex education to generate more applications from qualified, full pay students of both sexes, or be willing to accept single sex applicants of inferior quality due to the declining numbers of males (or females) applying to their schools. These schools prided themselves on their academic superiority, so diluting the product was not an option. Trying to stem the tide of runaway inflation and escalating tuition costs was not realistic. Nearly every all-male school acquiesced and began to accept alumni daughters and other interested female applicants, while most of the all-girls schools and military schools decided to stay the course in the name of doing what their alumnae and alumni preferred.

The next challenge all these schools faced, once they'd made the decision about the make-up of their schools, was how they would pay for that new reality. Remember that private schools were "endowment and tuition driven," so losing net tuition revenue because of higher costs and having fewer applicants meant that now a school had to reach out to its alumni for even greater support. Consider the position of the all-boys schools' capital campaigns when compared to the all-girls' and military schools and the realities of fund-raising. The general rule of thumb is that well-to-do people give to success, not failure. They may bail you out from a disastrous situation once, but they want to feel as though they are backing winners. Additionally, nearly 50 years ago decisions about philanthropy were being made predominately by men, and the beneficiaries were their schools and colleges. The only exception to this rule may have been the most prominent of the all-girls schools, whose successful alumnae credited their schools for much of their success in life and drove the philanthropy dollars in their direction.

The schools that were now co-educational had the opportunity to solicit both alumni whose sons could benefit from the school they loved, as well as alumni whose daughters could now benefit. Furthermore, given the environment in the Seventies with a number of formerly "closed clubs" for men now being opened to women, there were many families, in addition to those in a school's alumni database, who wanted their female offspring to have the opportunity so long denied to them. These newly created coed schools had the perfect opportunity to provide for the future with large endowment campaigns — and most of them did.

The all-girls schools and military schools actually found themselves, relatively speaking, in a deficit position: they were going to continue to be challenged in the admissions process since they were swimming against a numbers tide by limiting their applicants' gender. Furthermore, in the private school community, having resources from a strong and successful admissions pipeline, and having the use of supplementary income from an endowment, allowed schools to address failing infrastructure issues, to offer increasingly important financial aid, and to build and offer new programs. If a school had limited resources, it was going to have trouble competing. This, ironically, became known as the "Arms Race" — building better athletic facilities, better libraries, and nicer dormitories.

In 1939, famed LIFE Magazine photographer Alfred Eisenstaedt took a series of photographs on Culver's campus for a photo essay in the magazine. This shot features a battalion commander senior officer (at right) advising a new cadet in the Legion Memorial Building. An additional photograph from the series is shown on page 12.

All things considered, the handful of all-girls schools and military schools that survived deserve great credit. They were swimming, to extend the metaphor, against the tide and swimming uphill during the decade of the 1970s. Many schools could not manage the challenge and they folded. Others reinvented themselves to fill niches in the education space not available heretofore. That may have been the reason for the ad about sending your broken children to military school, so they could be "repaired." Some schools decided to focus their outreach to families with children diagnosed with learning and processing challenges. The advent of computers meant that any school could retrain its staff to meet the increasing needs of children with different learning styles. There were many casualties of the social revolution of the decade of the Seventies: drug use, sexual promiscuity, and the rebellion against previously accepted behavioral norms; all of these realities translated into rehabilitation opportunities for schools looking for students. Additionally, the "discovery" or realization that many children who had been unsuccessful in school were struggling with learning differences — especially dyslexia — and all these children needed schools to attend which would support them with these challenges.

Culver students conduct a discussion around the oval Harkness table, which encourages open-minded discussion with minimal teacher intervention.

The military school challenges were even more significant, so if other schools had it tough, military schools found themselves still trying to sell a better buggy whip while fighting a serious image problem because of the war in Vietnam. Their time-tested and time-honored model made sense to them and to their alumni, but if people were not buying buggy whips because they were now driving cars, it really didn't matter how whiz-bang their buggy whip was. Herein lay the problem and the ultimate challenge — could military school education as envisioned by Col. Fleet and Gen. Gignilliat be relevant in today's educational and social landscape?

CULVER

IN THE GREAT WAR OF 1914 – 1918
THESE SONS OF CULVER GAVE TO THEIR COUNTRY
THE UTMOST MEASURE OF PATRIOTIC DEVOTION
THAT LIBERTY SHOULD NOT PERISH FROM THE EARTH

ALBERT WILLARD ANGELL	BOTHWELL BIERCE KANE
FRANK HOLMES ATLEE	MYRON ALEXANDER KENNY
PIERCE BUTLER ATWOOD	HENRY HALLOCK KERR
RAYMOND BROOKS AUSTIN	JOHN HENRY KOENIG, JR.
EDWARD DAVID BAKER	EUGENE HANKIN KOTHE
GEORGE CARLYLE BAKER	GEORGE RIDER MASON
ROBERT HARRIS BARTLETT	ALEXANDER FERDINAND MATHEWS
JOSEPH ANTHONY BAUMER	GUINN WHITEHURST MATTERN
ERNEST FRANKLIN BLEULER	ARTHUR BEAMER McCORMICK
WILLIAM CARL BROEKER	DONALD RAYMOND McGEE
CLARENCE BOOTH BROOKS	WILLIAM WESLEY McKELVEY
MALCOLM COTTON BROWN	JOHN ALLEN McMILLAN
...OWN	CHARLES BRUCE MURRAY
...CANARY	EVERETT EWING NOBLE
...ENER	RICHARD LUCIAN PAGE
...ARKE, JR.	JAMES SHRIGLEY PALMER
...AND COBURN	MAXWELL OSWALD PARRY
...DAVIDSON	PERCY ROBERT PRESTON
...DOUGLAS, JR.	EDWARD DAVID PRICHARD
...ORGAN DRAPER	RICHARD BRUMBACK REED
...T DUANE	RICHARD HARRISON RISTINE
...S DUNCAN	RODERICK WILLIAM ROMBAUER
...H EBERHARDT, JR.	HAROLD GEORGE ROSS
...ARR	RALPH AUGUSTUS RUSSELL
...XANDER FLEET	JOHN GEORGE SCHNEIDER, JR.
...BE FOORD	EDWARD STANLEIGH...
...MOND FORRESTER	DUNLAP ORIS SI...
...AS FRANKLIN	CLARENCE FAIR...
...AZIER	EBEN LE ROY S...
	WILLIAM EVER...
	CLARENCE JO...
	McCREA STEP...
	WILLIS DANIE...
	JAMES JEFFE...
	WILLIAM CL...
	CHARLES HE...
	JAMES LIVIN...
	ELLIS LOBA...
	WILLIAM E...
	ORVIL...
	JO...

...AROL...

A...

Chapter Three: Do the Right Thing, Always

The historical documents from Culver had convinced me that this proud Academy had executed its educational plan beautifully for over seventy years. The other competing reality was that the original plan was straining under the weight of a model that teetered in the balance and was increasingly having to apologize for its relative lack of success off and on for the next 30 years. There existed a dozen or so better known, mainly New England boarding schools that had all embraced coeducation as the answer to their early 1970s challenges. They had accepted applications from girls, built their female presence strategically, and moved quickly from a 90:10 ratio in the first year of admitting girls to a 50:50 coeducational balance a decade or so later. They had asked their alumni to support this bold and important experiment to ensure the future of their beloved school, and they had built financial war chests that would support them when the financial times became more challenging. They had also used their resources to position themselves for success with pristine campuses, significant endowments that allowed them to admit without concern about financial wherewithal, and cutting edge academic programs and new buildings that showcased their offerings. New libraries graced their campuses. New gyms and athletic facilities were built, and close behind them, new Arts and Performance Centers. The "arms race" was on by the mid-1980s, and it was clear which schools had chosen the best strategy.

Fortunately for Culver, this Academy, like many of the successful eastern prep schools mentioned above that had been conceived of and built by a family with a vision for developing leaders for our relatively new democracy, had engaged in almost all the strategic moves highlighted above. In 1971 Culver made the right decision about admitting girls and ventured boldly into coeducation, in spite of the fact that the place and role of women in the military was completely uncertain and not universally accepted. Culver realized that admitting girls to the Academy as full partners was essential for philosophical and educational, as well as financial reasons, but Culver was even more thoughtful than these other schools because Culver understood that any school with a strong and specific heritage — whether it was an all-boys history or a military past — should not ask the newcomers to compete for relevance in that time honored tradition. Culver decided, instead, that its girls needed their own special traditions, so there would be no primary and secondary gender designations in a military system with the power of tradition behind it. The girls would learn leadership, but they would look to their own leaders, not necessarily to the boys. Box #1…move to a coeducational program — check.

Left: Students contemplate the legacy of service of the 86 Culver graduates who made the ultimate sacrifice during World War I, and whose names are immortalized on the Gold Star wall of the Legion Memorial Building.

The beginning of another important tradition: the first Culver Academy for Girls (today's Culver Girls Academy) graduation in 1972.

Jim Henderson '52 and Jim Dicke '64 were leaders in the milestone Choices for Culver campaign.

Culver had also used this opportunity to build a significant endowment. Two earlier campaigns in the 1960s and 1970s had raised $5 million and $18 million, respectively. The Choices for Culver campaign in the 1980s was co-chaired by two graduates: one, a Culver native and prominent Fortune 500 business leader; the other an Ohio native and young alumnus who was building what has become one of America's foremost manufacturing concerns. Both men had a passion for the school and a deep appreciation for its history and place in American secondary education. One was the son of one of Culver's longest serving faculty members, so his perspective of having known Culver then and now lent considerable credibility to the Campaign. People had trusted his father when he was the Admissions Director in the 1930s, '40s and '50s and they trusted him now. When the Campaign ended on December 31, 1988, Culver had raised more money than any other secondary boarding school ever had (Note: Phillips Andover Academy held the standing record of $54,000,000 set in 1979). The Choices for Culver campaign goal was $47 million; however, in order to prove it never took a backseat to the Eastern Prep Goliaths, Culver pushed its Campaign receipts to $60,100,000. The intrepid and inspirational leaders of the effort were Jim Henderson '52 and Jim Dicke '64. Box #2...Build a significant endowment — check.

A member of the founding family, the Culver family of St. Louis, had discovered Culver's pristine location on the shores of one of Indiana's second largest natural lakes — Lake Maxinkuckee. He decided that this was the place to build his dream project if only he could decide what that project would be. After a number of unsuccessful ventures, he landed on the perfect solution: a school for young men. He recalls feeling inspired by the place and experiencing an almost spiritual serenity when he was there. His vision was "his castle in the air," and his family dedicated its resources to building out a school on this beautiful 1800-acre tract. Box #3... beautiful and spacious campus — check.

Culver had also determined that the strategy of "build it and they will come" made sense. The school was operating in a different part of the country and was not competing directly with the Eastern Prep schools for talent. While that was true, Culver was competing against the successful and academically-strong high schools of the Midwest; and not only did those highly-regarded public schools and private day schools have strong academic programs, they had excellent extracurricular and athletic resources and facilities as well, meaning that Culver's was competing with students' home town schools — a reality that was not the case with many of the eastern preps. So, Jim Henderson led the Board in a campaign to commit considerable resources to the refreshment of the Academy's beautiful campus and its physical plant.

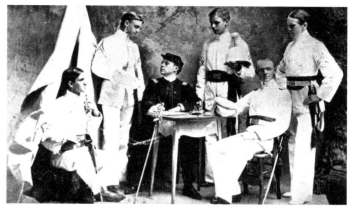

The first cadets of Culver, pictured in 1894.

The one thing the school had not done was to opt out of its commitment to offering the American, more behaviorally based model of education that had distinguished the school throughout its early history. Culver had decided, in all its collective Board wisdom, that what differentiated Culver from all the other prep schools in the country was its singular brand of military-style education. Yes, it could try to become the Andover or Exeter of the Midwest, but that is not what it aspired to be — a version of someone else's dream. Culver wanted only to be CULVER, and it wanted to be the best version of itself.

The early 1990s-constructed Huffington Library, left, enhanced the classic beauty of the Culver campus, as did the Roberts Hall of Science and Dicke Hall of Mathematics (right), opened in 2002. In the center is the storied Eppley Hall of Humanities, dating to the 1950s.

The Board announced its decision to retain its identity as a military academy a decade before Pam and I were introduced to this special place. The precipitating event requiring this public declaration was the formation of an administrative committee in 1985, The Committee on the Culver Experience, that had debated changing the Culver brand from Military to Corporate. Might military uniforms be exchanged for blue blazers, striped ties, and grey slacks? Might the style of the signature Culver boys' leadership program now be modeled on the office and the boardroom?

The committee was chaired by two senior faculty members, and the collective experience of the committee members brought over 200 years of service to Culver. Their issue was not that they did not value what the military model could do. Their issue was the difficulty they were having selling the model to the modern teenage boy.

Given this challenge, they may have used a rationale that went something like this: Since the girls were using a non-military model of leadership and were having an excellent experience, why couldn't the boys do the same?

This thought process from the committee was shared by Ralph Manuel with the Board, and it was not without some merit. There were those Board members who saw the value in such a move. However, most of the leadership of the Board, all men who had attended the Academy in the 1940s and 1950s, were adamant that if Culver strayed from its signature philosophy, it would get lost in the wash of boarding and day schools that all were trying to do the same thing — educating without serious regard for the education of the "whole child."

Culver's Board did not want to be responsible for taking away from their school the most distinctive and impactful aspect of Culver Military Academy…its traditions and leadership program. These Board members felt strongly that replacing the military program at Culver would be tantamount to eliminating Culver's chance to differentiate itself. Even though there were concerns about flagging enrollment numbers, the Board stood firm, believing the system could be enhanced and made relevant again. Theirs was a courageous decision; there was much at risk here.

It was not lost on me as I did my research on both Culver's history and on the current educational and sociological research on boys and their development, that history, as well as personalities, played a role in the success of institutions. I was not at that moment capable of assessing the importance of the backgrounds of the "Superintendents" or Presidents/Heads of School, but that could have been important in my understanding of the Academy's evolution and challenges. For example, during its 100 plus year history, one third of its Superintendents were men who had recently retired from a career in the military — General Delmar T. Spivey, General John Carpenter, General John Dobson, and Colonel Benjamin Barone — four of eleven; and one of the four lasted more than four years, suggesting that General Spivey was the outlier in this approach.

On three other occasions, the Superintendent came from the ranks of Culver Military Academy, having served as members of the Administration for years before being chosen to lead the Academy — General Leigh Gignilliat, Colonel W.E. Gregory, and John Mars. All had served in the military, and each had served Culver for a significant amount of time before taking the reins. These three men had come to understand and embrace Culver's traditions well before having to make important, leadership decisions about its educational philosophy and its future. All three were extremely successful, suggesting this was the recipe for success. Only twice had the Superintendents come to Culver having served as a leader of other military schools — Reverend John McKenzie, the first Superintendent, and Colonel Alexander Fleet. Reverend McKenzie's tenure was short-lived. He wanted to change the name of the Academy from Culver Academy to St. Paul's School, and, furthermore, he was a proponent of the military model of education he had practiced at his previous school. Henry Harrison Culver, the founder, made the decision to relieve McKenzie of his duties less than a year into his term. Fleet was an excellent choice to succeed McKenzie and became an exemplary leader for Culver.

The only other person to lead Culver during its 105-year history was the man whose retirement was creating this opportunity for Pam and me. Dr. Ralph Manuel had been an officer in the U.S. Navy, as well as the Dean of Dartmouth College. He was a seasoned, educational leader when he arrived at Culver, and he led the Academy through many important changes and program improvements during his 17-year tenure. He, too, was committed to Culver's approach, but he was beginning to view the military decision from a practical rather than a philosophical vantage point. He wanted Culver to succeed, and he believed that moving from the military model to something more agreeable to male applicants was the pathway there. He never said this to me, and he never disparaged the model the Academy had chosen to follow.

Culver's 11th Superintendent, Ralph Manuel (who served from 1982-1999)

Understanding the profile of the most successful leaders of the Academy might have convinced me that having a combination of military training and experience in addition to school experience (especially at Culver) was the key to success, having a truer understanding of the mores and values of Culver. Since I did not possess either, it may have been fortunate that I was not aware of these "prerequisites."

I also was unaware, as I began my search for answers to the challenges of the school we would be leading, of the societal shifts that were taking place as we marched, no pun intended, toward this new responsibility. The image of the military had been tarnished almost irretrievably during the Vietnam War. The draft system had become something to avoid, and the notion of "serving one's Country" felt hollow and uninviting to many. There were issues about draft dodgers and conscientious objectors. People growing up in the post-Vietnam decades of the 1970s and 1980s had been raised to question the integrity, mentality, and morality of those in uniform, and very few people believed war was a noble undertaking.

By the 1990s things had begun to change for the better for the military, but it was hard to assess whether the mood and attitudes about the military in the country were changing or were simply not topics of conversation. There were a few well-publicized military "engagements" around the world, but mostly the American military operated in secrecy. I remember being told once during the decade of the 1980s that we had a military presence in 300 countries, but many of them were places the average citizen had never heard of. The military re-booted in obscurity. People only had hangover images of what war was. The national parades during these years had been watered down, and people were expressing far less respect for the American flag. There was, however, the resilience of a few military leaders in the persons of Generals Norman Schwarzkopf and Colin Powell.

In the world of education, anyone who thought it was a good idea to study Civics or to follow a curriculum that outlined the values and specifics of "our American Democratic Heritage," was deemed inappropriate and archaic. People stopped pledging Allegiance to the United States of America, and 4th of July celebrations were more about the fireworks than patriotism. Finally, people who were promoting time-honored values and virtues were considered anti-intellectual, dangerously conservative, and hopelessly out of date or fashion.

This was the environment we were in as I hunkered down in my graduate school mode to look for clues and then answers to some extremely important questions and challenges that we were certain to face when we began at Culver. With a superficial understanding of the history of Culver, an incredibly positive impression of the governance team on the Board, and a good feeling about the qualities and strength of the alumni, the students, and the faculty and staff, I delved into all the research I could find to see if there were opinions about and then support for the idea of utilizing the military model to teach leadership to adolescent and teenage boys in an academic setting in the New Millennium. To do this I was going to have to understand how and why this institution had survived and thrived for so long and then to determine how it could recapture the brilliance of its past in the current political, educational, and social environment we were in now.

It occurred to me more than once that Pam and I were making a major life decision based on a great deal of intuition and by trusting our instincts and experience. While it was true that we had been living the "school life" for nearly 30 years, while we spoke the language of schools, and while we certainly understood what quality education was and could ferret out dysfunction when we saw it, we had very little firm knowledge and understanding about our destination. Someone asked me how it felt to be changing course almost completely this late in our lives, pulling up stakes from the eastern boarding school community and heading to a military school — whatever that meant — in the Midwest. My answer was as follows: I am told that when you have released your hold from the trapeze and are waiting for the other trapeze to come back to you…while you are flying or floating through the air — you either experience exhilaration or abject terror. We felt exhilarated at the prospect of going to Culver. Now, we were going to need to find reasons that validated the viability of a military leadership model of education.

One of the reasons I had enrolled in a graduate program at age 50 was so I could link up educational theory with practice. I had been well educated, and I had spent almost three decades teaching, coaching, and being an administrator. What I was missing was the theory that buttressed all my practical experience. Usually, one is introduced to intellectual or educational frameworks and theory in graduate school.

My graduate coursework had been strictly in my discipline (English) and had been limited to summer school study that included a few literature and poetry courses, which I sandwiched in between the end of the school year and the beginning of fall sports practices. I couldn't wait to add another dimension to the way I thought about education, especially now that I was looking into an approach to education with which I was totally unfamiliar.

I discovered two approaches to thinking about Culver's educational model that I believed would be instructive almost immediately. I had had virtually no experience with literary reviews, but I learned quickly what a treasure trove "lit reviews" were for graduate students doing research. It was like "Googling" a topic, but instead of getting someone's thoughts on the topic, you were introduced to the reviews of the literature/research on the subject. Then you could head to the library and read the reviews. By studying them you could determine what was of interest and use, and soon you had "warrants" for the opinions and declarations you made in your research papers.

I began my research on military models of leadership. There was a great deal about college ROTC programs, Officer Candidate Schools' educational approaches, and the four Service Academies. I needed to refine the filter. Military models for boys? Two studies came to the fore: one on "prosocial behavior" and the other on the military model as a way of teaching leadership. I had never heard of prosocial behavior, but it was almost self-explanatory. If you were prosocial, you were positive in your social actions. Clearly, this was the opposite of anti-social, which seemed to be the descriptor some military schools were using to describe the students they sought to educate or re-educate. I hoped these study topics would provide a foundation for my understanding of the type of school I would be leading.

A memorable and hallowed space in the campus area known as Main Guard: an exhibit honoring the five recipients of the Congressional Medal of Honor who attended Culver.

But immediately, I sensed a disconnect. The studies on prosocial behavior were mainly conducted on boys described as "troubled," and that was not the sense we had of the students we had met at Culver. Culver's students were bright-eyed, curious, respectful, and not needing rehabilitation any more than the students at our former school, a prestigious Eastern boarding school. I catalogued the salient underpinnings of prosocial behavior and moved on to the second of these studies — the military as a leadership model — in hopes of finding material to advance my thinking on this construct.

The two studies above were not the only models I was researching. I was also looking deeply into organizational behavior, institutional communication, leadership styles, and management systems. Remember, my research question was tending toward why a school that had made all the appropriate decisions to prepare it to be successful in the 21st century was not seeing the same high level of success as some other schools that had made thoughtful and timely decisions about their futures were enjoying. Culver was judged by most observers and by most standards to be successful, but the accepted measures of success used to identify the truly successful secondary boarding schools were not as strong as Culver.

There is an old saying used by horsemen and horsewomen to describe the challenge of getting your horse to do what you want it to do:

> If your horse does not do what you ask it to do, either you are asking the wrong question, or you are asking the question wrong.

I believe I was doing both. Unfortunately, I did not have the knowledge and experience then that would have made this research challenge more informative to me. Pam and I had been given sound bites, admissions videos, mission statements, and student handbooks and statements of philosophy on matters such as discipline and military protocols. But Culver still existed in a vacuum for us since we had no direct experience. This meant that the knowledge I was seeking and needed to validate on the use of the military model as an approach to developing leadership in young men, on the grounds that it was not only defensible but also more successful than other educational approaches, was difficult for me to put into a useful context. Culver had many narratives suggesting that its claims were justified, but I needed both theory and practical proof to support these stories.

I discovered that the precepts and outcomes of the military model were almost the same as those promoted as the positive outcomes from "prosocial" behavior. For example, the military system uses a program of graduated responsibility and graduated privilege to teach personal responsibility. The military model also believes that the setting and celebrations of personal milestones as a vehicle for building the confidence and courage one needs to lead are critically important to a young man's development. The military uses extrinsic awards and rewards to develop a commitment to intrinsic values. The military model stresses communication, teamwork, and an entrepreneurial approach to problem-solving. Most important, the military model understands that the system needs to be set up to recruit a young man to maturation and responsibility. The military approach stresses personal responsibility and accountability, so it underscores and rewards young people for acting on these principles. These were definitely the language and the processes of prosocial behavior as well.

As a teacher and a coach of teenagers, I saw the similarities between building up young men, using the military model and what I had done, or tried to do, for three decades, using my more experienced participants to encourage and train those newest to the team builds leadership skills and follower skills. I even had the practice of handing out lollipops to those who performed in accordance with the values and virtues we supported as a program or a group as a way of underscoring this behavior.

I began to see a pathway, but, again, I had only concepts with which to work, not practice.

Chapter Four: Education is not Preparation for Life; Education is Life Itself (John Dewey)

I had six months to make sense of this new and fascinating approach to education, and, fortunately, I had the latitude to study and to write about those topics that would help build my theoretical knowledge about the philosophy and the administrative realities, as well as the narratives and symbols of Culver. You could say I had two of the most important tools necessary to prepare myself for success as a new Head of School. What I was missing was context, and in my experience, context is everything. I had spent my first 29 years after college in a traditional, well-resourced, tony, private boarding school in New England. Our two children had attended and graduated from the School, and it was all we had ever known. I had served as director of college advising, director of admissions, and vice rector (COO) as well as having taught, coached, and run two different dormitories for many of the years we were there. I understood this model of education and believed it made sense. After all, this is how successful schools operated: Choose able and motivated students, challenge them intellectually, train their minds and their bodies, and provide for their well-being emotionally and physically.

The educational philosophy was anchored in the best of English boarding school traditions: choose the best possible candidates, surround them with talented and responsible adults, provide them with a challenging curriculum, organize games (athletics) for them, and enrich their souls and characters through a schedule of chapel services and community service. This was, once again, a version of the Etonian model: provide the flower with enough sun and water, and it will blossom on its own. General structure sets the boundaries, but the student needs to develop his (or her) talents by exercising freedom within that structure. Students were encouraged to experiment with approaches to learning to determine what worked best for them individually. The rules were minimal — 1) don't lie, (2) cheat, or (3) steal. Don't (4) use banned substances; and finally, (5) do your own work. In other words, "You're a smart kid, figure it out."

Now we were heading to a school that believed in training its students intentionally to do the right thing...always; and to build the habits necessary to live one's life as a person of character and a responsibility, one upon whom others could depend. There would be aspects of military drill, Aristotelian habituation — "We are what we habitually do" — and codification, meaning one size truly does fit all. There was a book of rules, infinitely long and specific. There were monitored study halls proctored by older student leaders and "assisted" by faculty members on duty in the girls' dorms, or, in the boys' barracks. Students had lights out and morning reveille. They were obligated to clean ("police") their rooms every morning, except Saturday, and then the room was inspected. Cleaning one's room was no more a matter of personal choice than was wearing the uniform of the day properly, which meant uniformly, respectfully, and well. There were graduated ranks and privileges according to age and performance; and academic excellence and personal citizenship mattered if one planned to progress in the system.

This was a world apart from the school we had grown up in. Students there were encouraged to clean their rooms, maybe weekly, if they would…please. They determined when they needed to study and when they needed to go to bed. There was a morning Chapel requirement at 8:00 a.m., four mornings a week, and it was mandatory. Students there had to play sports, go to class, dress comfortably, but always neatly and cleanly; and attend a few seated, family-style meals a week. There were precious few requirements about the "how" of things; rather, most of the direction involved the "what." The "how" was something you had to work out on your own or with the support of faculty or friends.

These two school philosophies were in many ways diametrically opposed, but each had a connection to the concept that being a person of good character mattered if you were going to have a good life. For our eastern prep school, the connection was being a "good Christian." For Culver the concept was being a good practitioner of your faith or moral philosophy and a good citizen, and, if you had the requisite skill set, a good leader. They were almost nothing alike, but in many ways foundationally similar. One used a military model for the boys and a prefect system for the girls, and the other used the Church-school model to shape its values. The difference was in the understanding of how one gets to the destination point.

This conceptual schism was at first problematic. Our lens had been eastern prep. We had become comfortable with the concept that children learn well if given a sense of responsibility for finding their own way. Trial and error could be a good teacher, especially for those who were genetically leaning toward being responsible. If they didn't do their homework and go to class and get a failing grade for the day, they would understand that actions have consequences; and the next time they most likely would do the homework, unless, of course, they are very bright and could manage to finesse the fact that they did not open their book the night before class. Then they learned that they were smart enough to get away with not preparing for class — a dangerous lesson.

This may be a trivial example, but if we up the ante and discuss

The Minerva or Athena sculpture known for generations as "The Spirit of Culver" (seen also on page 50) was a gift of the class of 1929. An early and iconic visual feminine representation on Culver's campus, it was the work of artist Helen Doft.

the concept of older students taking responsibility for younger students, the point I am making is more impactful. There is a history in English schools of using older students to supervise and counsel the younger boys, and it is called "proctoring." Although the model made sense conceptually, for years in these schools there was a problem with the older boys bullying or hazing or directing those younger boys (or girls) to do the older students' bidding. Regardless of this history, and in an effort to curtail this unfortunate activity, boarding schools in this country attempted to eliminate the hazing problem by assigning the older boys the duty of looking out for the younger boys and being responsible for them. The proctoring or prefect system worked well for awhile, but the older boys soon realized that the less they interfered with the younger boys' lives, the more popular they were. The older boys discovered that "he who governs least, governs best." And so, the system in these eastern prep schools lapsed into mediocrity, just as the English system had. This may have been another reminder that careful and serious people understand that one needs to inspect what he or she expects.

When we arrived at our first school, it employed a proctor system for the youngest boys — 7th and 8th graders — but the distinction between the younger boys and the older boys blurred over time and there was a point in the early 1970s when the notion of being my "younger" brother's keeper went quickly out of fashion. The adolescent world became an all-for-one world in which age and grade mattered little.

Not so in a military system, especially at Culver. Culver's educational system was based on the American model I referenced earlier. Training, the principles of citizenship and leadership, and clearly articulated systems of rank and promotion in a meritocratic context

The Gold Star Ceremony on Memorial Day, led by CMA cadets and CGA girls, in an event honoring Culver's Gold Star men who lost their lives in service to their country.

mattered and needed to be adhered to if young boys were to develop into young men. There was no "create your own adventure" at Culver. You did not have the opportunity to determine what pathways you wanted to follow unless you had first mastered the requirements and developed the habits of a responsible citizen. Culver still believed that behavior was conditioned by repetition and reinforcement. Aristotle reminded us that "we are what we repeatedly do." If I practice being the person I want to be, I will be more likely to become that person. If I challenge myself, or if I am challenged by the system, to do those things that are necessary but are also things I would rather not do, I will become better at taking care of all manner of business. If I am required to greet people in the hall and acknowledge their name and rank, I will develop a lifelong habit of acknowledging people respectfully.

Our two children, both alumni of our eastern boarding school, are wonderful young adults — responsible and responsive; thoroughly educated, and service-oriented.

Many of the alumni of their institution are also impressive adults doing wonderful things in their lives. Clearly, the eastern model could and did work for many students, which meant that we had to look at any comparison, not as a zero-sum game, but as different approaches to the same destination. We were not interested in making our new school into our former school. The Trustees of Culver had been perfectly clear about that. They believed in what Culver was doing and were interested only in making it even more successful. However, we did have to provide an honest assessment of the new model, so we could determine what adjustments to make and which themes to tweak, to ensure the outcomes Culver was determined to achieve.

What we had known for almost three decades back East was certainly part of our educational DNA, so our former school was always going to be a point of reference. Fortunately, I had served in four administrative roles within the school, and in each position, my mission was to improve the processes and outcomes of the office. I believe that gave me a certain objectivity when it came to evaluating and assessing both the parts and the whole of any school. What we knew was clear. What we would come to understand was totally unexpected.

For example, eastern prep schools generally house members of the faculty in the dormitories as heads of houses, responsible for the lives of the thirty or so students in their care. Additionally, these faculty members teach and coach, completing what had been called the "triple threat" model. These adults live in the same building as the students do, or in attached homes. They are technically "on duty" but they are not always present. They might be preparing for the next day's classes or putting their own children to bed. They spend the evening in the dorm, having checked the students in at the curfew hour — usually 11:00 p.m.

New cadets are trained by their elder peers during orientation at the start of the 2013-2014 school year. Culver's leadership model emphasizes personal responsibility and duty to one's self as well as the larger unit or dorm.

At Culver, on the other hand, the cadet and girls' leaders take responsibility for the order and well-being of the barracks and dormitories in the evening. There is a faculty or staff member on duty during the academic study period — C.Q. (closed quarters) — but that person leaves the barracks to the student leaders when C.Q. ends at 11:00 p.m. There is an apartment or two for faculty or staff members in the residence halls, but the adults who live there are present in case of an emergency (fire or illness) and have no specific responsibility for the care and feeding of the students. The person who has the responsibility for the well-being of the students at Culver is the "counselor," who foremost serves as a counselor, not a "triple threat" employee. The counselor serves as the nexus for all aspects of a student's life. The counselor is available all day long to support students, i.e., he or she is not away teaching, coaching, or doing administrative duties; and is on-call at night, just not necessarily in the barracks or dorms. (*Note: In addition to the counselor as a support person, the boys have "military mentors" and the girls have "resident directors" to provide additional adult presence and guidance).

You can imagine my surprise the first time I "stood B.I." (Barracks Inspection) in the Band. I arrived at 7 p.m. and was met at the door by a cadet leader who greeted me professionally, introduced himself, and explained to me that he was the Unit Duty Officer (UDO) for the night. He told me he would do an "accountability check" to make certain every cadet was where he was supposed to be to begin C.C.Q., and then he would check in with me every time he did his rounds of the barracks on the half hour to make sure cadets were studying and otherwise doing what was asked of them. He continued to explain that if there was an issue with noise or of cadets being out of their rooms, he would be in his room and would appreciate my alerting him so he could handle and correct the matter. I was accustomed to being the only responsible person in the dorm back East, so this was remarkable. Students' taking responsibility for other students and taking responsibility for the well-being of the system at Culver struck me as something I could certainly work with, happily.

These contradictory approaches and philosophies complicated my universe of understanding for the next six months. Every time I learned something new about Culver, I would overlay it on my experience as a teacher and administrator for the past three decades to determine how well it fit my educational philosophy. I must admit it was a challenge, but the biggest hurdle was the fact that I had not yet experienced Culver myself, and I was learning that Culver is a hard place to explain.

The topic I was unwittingly attempting to unpack was what did schools need to do to realize their full potential. I said earlier in this book that I was certain that "context was everything." I had also been taught by a strong head of school that your mission must drive every decision you make and that ideology mattered. You determined your destination and set down the principles and values that would inform your decision making along the way; and then you acted on your intentions, consistently. Whether the eastern boarding schools had chosen an English public-school model rather than the more behavioral American model, it really shouldn't matter. I would imagine that relatively few people could even make or comprehend such a distinction. What people cared about was the quality of the educational offerings, the demand statistics, admissions competitiveness, college placement — and the culture of the school. Whether it was more or less behavioral in its approach was surely secondary. Whether the students had a dress code or not didn't matter that much in the final analysis.

There are great coaches who are dictatorial and loud, just as there are successful coaches who are understated and consensual in their approach. There are players' coaches and organization coaches, and both win Super Bowls or World Series and national championships. There is not a right way or a wrong way; you just have to do what you do well. And then you have to find a way to explain who you are and why you operate as you do. That second part was not going to be easy.

I was already beginning to understand the difficulty of explaining the military model as something that would benefit young men, because there did not seem to be anyone who had created an acceptable elevator speech to explain it fully or satisfactorily. Since it appeared to be a throwback or an antiquated way of organizing Generation X and Y adolescents, any description had to be crisp and relevant. If you fumbled around the subject or started with "What we are not," all was already lost.

I recall sitting in my office a few months after our arrival with two of the most influential trustees at Culver — both graduates — who lived in the Midwest; ran successful, national companies; sat on college boards of trustees; and did much of their work on the East Coast. I asked each of them whether they often brought up the fact that they had gone to Culver at meetings or dinner parties back East. Both responded, somewhat embarrassed, that no, they did not. It took too long to explain Culver, they said; and people already had too many preconceived notions about military schools to even begin to open their minds.

Students from Culver Girls Academy and Culver Military Academy share the campus and many of its experiences, though the girls' school was designed to be intentionally coordinate, holding a separate identity and structure from that of the boys — rather than simply coeducational.

Many years after Pam and I had arrived in this special, inexplicable place, I was touring a head of schools around the campus at Culver. He had recently come to the Midwest to run an excellent day school. He had heard about Culver and wanted to visit. He and I walked around the campus for almost an hour, and his eyes were literally popping out of his head. "I had no idea what a magnificent campus Culver had. I am absolutely blown away," he said. Later, as we sat talking in my office, which he remarked "has to be the most impressive Head of Schools' office in the country," he asked if he could ask a candid question. Certainly. "I just don't get the military thing. Does it really work?" I had just finished regaling him with the virtues and values of our leadership systems at Culver, and he still had no concept of what I was talking about. It may be true that "those who attended Culver cannot explain it; and those who did not, cannot possibly understand it."

The military was the lightning rod, and there were so many things about it that cut against the eastern model grain. For example, Culver had not dived into coeducation in the traditional way. In 1971, Culver did not simply add girls to the mix and hope they would be accepted and fit in over time. Culver believed that the military model, while extremely important for the growth and development of boys and young men, was not as appropriate for girls. So, they looked to a more traditional boarding school model for their young women, believing that girls needed and deserved their own traditions and stories. Culver created the Culver Academy for Girls, which after a few years was renamed Culver Girls Academy (CGA).

If things were not difficult enough to explain with the military, now Culver had to explain whether it was one school or two — CMA and CGA. And only making matters worse, there was also the Culver Summer Schools and Camps, which was actually a combination of summer leadership experiences organized around a six-week summer camp model that used the military framework for both boys and girls, and that taught many of the same lessons taught in the winter school — in CMA and CGA.

There was a lot to sort out here, but in good Culver fashion, as I would soon learn, there was a unanimity of thought about what each of these organizations, or as I saw them, pieces of the puzzle that was Culver, was tasked to do: Prepare young people for leadership and responsible citizenship by educating the whole person — mind, body, and spirit.

Culver had as compelling a mission statement as any school in the country, and over its hundred plus years of educating young people, it had graduated more than its share of extremely successful, productive, and good people. Still, it was not well known; it was certainly not fully understood; and it was exactly the school young people in today's world needed...in spite of the fact that the eastern establishment could not possibly understand or embrace its value proposition. Culver was doing so much right, but it was not being viewed, treated, or valued as it should have been. This was going to be fun. I channeled the educational philosopher who had, no doubt, influenced the thinking of Culver's early leaders:

> Give pupils something to do, not something to learn; and the doing is of such a nature as to demand thinking; learning naturally results.

Chapter Five: We are What We Repeatedly Do — Aristotle

I finished my coursework for my Ph.D., but I had to put the dissertation on hold, since I expected I would be devoting myself 24/7 to our new adventure. Culver was a large and complex institution, and with both Summer Schools and Winter Schools — yes, plural — we would have plenty to do. I had experienced four major leadership transitions in our former school, and I understood firsthand how challenging and time consuming a process these handoffs could be. Some have compared it to a new stepfather or stepmother coming into a family. Everyone was used to the old way of seeing and experiencing the world, and now there were new rhythms and a new head of the family. This created anxiety, hope, fear, and optimism all at once — for Culver and for us.

My initial assignment as the new Head of Schools was to review a Statement of Principles and Objectives Jim Henderson had written as part of the Schools' development of an updated Mission Statement. Jim asked me to read the document carefully and then contact him, so we could discuss both what I particularly liked about the Statement and what I believed needed to be changed. The first thing that impressed me was how similar it was to the original statements of mission created by the earliest leaders of the Academy. Next, I was impressed that a Board Chairman had taken personal responsibility for writing such a document. Finally, and most important, I was pleased to be asked to provide my perspective as the newcomer so that he and I could begin to work in partnership in leading the school. As it turned out, there was not much on which we disagreed. This would not be the only time Jim Henderson would teach me important things about Culver "by doing."

My first real on the ground experience, however, occurred a few weeks before we were officially scheduled to assume my responsibilities as Head of Schools. Given what I had learned about the summer program, and considering the strong recommendation Jim Henderson had made about our seeing the start of the summer program in person, I thought it wise to fly out to Culver and observe the opening of the Summer Schools and Camps. On this visit, I truly wanted to be the proverbial "fly on the wall." My plan was to learn by walking around. Yogi Berra was quoted as having said that "it is amazing how much you can see by just observing." I wanted to see this aspect of the Culver experience — this legendary Summer School — in action. Since there was no schedule for me, I decided to start my first day at Culver by sitting down for breakfast unobtrusively in the Woodcraft Camp Dining Hall. I went through the

Left: The rich tradition, precision, and pageantry of the Woodcraft Camp Drum & Bugle Corps is accentuated by the colorful Drum Major uniform during a summer garrison parade.

Horsemanship has been part of Culver's summer programming since 1907, and has involved young women since the first girls' summer program in 1965.

cafeteria line and headed to a table where four or five employees were eating. I did not introduce myself as their newly appointed "Superintendent." I introduced myself by name, got no response, and began to observe and listen. Three things became clear immediately: the camp systems were well-articulated and well-understood; the employees were all willing to do what was asked or needed from them; and the employees were Culver "through and through"— they identified with their School, even though they were summertime workers.

From there I headed to the welcoming and registration center housed in the Henderson Multi-Purpose Building. As I entered, I was reminded of a well-organized beehive. In spite of the overwhelming numbers of "campers" and families arriving on campus to register, everyone was in a line moving toward a table managed by smiling, professional, and well-informed Culver employees whose priorities were helpfulness, kindness, and efficiency. There were no long lines anywhere. The organization was incredible. Was this a military thing? If so, everyone should learn it. It was both re- spectful to the families and reassuring to the employees.

Next, I asked a few of the families going through the process to describe their experiences. Their responses were as uniform as the wardrobes of the employees and the Culver clothing the families were purchasing for their children (and themselves). The process was clearly well-organized; but it was also targeted and intentional. There was a plan at work, and after those new to camp had been registered; and once they had purchased all the uniforms and equipment they would need; and after they had been dropped off at their cabins or dormitories, they began preparing for what they would need to be able to do as members of this historic summer program. There was no sitting around. The Band began practicing for its first performance at that evening's introductory, all-camp meeting. Other groups of young men and women were practicing their marching, led by those who were returning to Culver for the third, fourth, fifth, or even ninth summer, and were now leading the process. Adults were stationed at the dormitories and cabins to welcome the newest members and to assure families that the training their nine- and ten-year-old children were engaged in was part of a process that would transform them into more mature and responsible young men and women during the next six weeks.

By eight o'clock that evening, every Woodcraft camper — ages 9–14 — (all 700 of them) and all Summer Upper Schoolers — ages 14–18 (all 650 of them) were marching toward the Academy's auditorium for their first official meeting. They marched in "units" with the newest members being led by their more experienced counterparts. The adults provided the safety nets for those least sure of themselves and those who needed more direction. This meeting, as with everything else I had seen during the day, had a specific purpose: to introduce all newcomers to the Culver Mission and remind returning campers of the importance of their leadership of the newer participants.

The themes were clear:

- We are many, but we are One Culver. (These young men and women came to Culver for the six-week summer program from 40 states and 30 countries and ages 9 through 18.)

- While we are here, we are here to do Culver. This is not a "create your own adventure" camp.

- Lastly, we expect from you the best you can give — in your effort, in your leadership, and in your character. You will get out of this experience exactly what you put into it; do not sell it or yourself short.

During the meeting, the individual "units" — Naval School Companies, Girls' School Decks, Aviation Wings, the School of Horsemanship units, and Girls' Horsemanship Deck in the Upper Schools — and Beavers and Cubs and for boys (a few years later, for both boys and girls), and Butterflies and Cardinals for girls in the Woodcraft Camp — cheered for themselves and for the other units. State and country flags were paraded on stage to celebrate the diversity of the campers, and new campers and Upper Schoolers learned the camp cheers. The student leader from the summer Upper Schools (referred to as the Regimental Commander) and the highest-ranking leader from the Woodcraft Camp (also a Regimental Commander) each addressed the entire auditorium of more than 1500 people and shared their aspirational and inspirational messages. Directors of the Camps and the Summer Program spoke as well, welcoming all to Culver and reinforcing the salient messages of leadership, service, and citizenship. I was thoroughly impressed by the consistency of and the obvious commitment to the messages being delivered.

Pam and I had not heard that much about the Summer Program during the interview and selection process, so this was an important puzzle piece for us to understand. The Summer School was only six weeks in length, which made it different from the Winter Schools — Culver Military Academy and Culver Girls' Academy — but it was part of the Culver program. It carried the Culver brand and was probably a good and accurate window into the philosophy and operations of The Academies. I returned home after a day and a half of observation, excited by the strength, relevance, and success of the summer version of Culver, especially impressed that this summer program had begun in 1902 and had been operating successfully for nearly 100 years.

The next three weeks passed quickly as Pam and I prepared to move permanently to Culver. We were both excited to begin this next chapter of our lives, and we were equally excited about what we were learning every day about this little known, but obviously special, school. An important part of our education on Culver came from nearly all 35 Board members and alumni from all places and all classes who wanted to congratulate us on the appointment, and in some cases, provide either context or helpful advice. Their letters were welcoming, grateful, and consistent in their commitment, loyalty, and willingness to help in any way they could. They also seemed to be expressing the unspoken hope that we would come to understand and love their school as they did. They were uniform in their belief that any successes they had had in their lives were due to the lessons learned at Culver and the guidance of their Culver faculty and staff.

Woodcraft girls passing in review, with sashes and guidons.

It had been 17 years since Culver had welcomed a new Head of School (formerly called the Superintendent, as the lead person is at West Point, the Naval Academy, the Air Force Academy, and the Coast Guard Academy) so the administrators still on campus a full month into the "summer" probably just assumed we could find our way around or possibly had not been informed about the timing of our arrival. Maybe they'd forgotten that new people needed orientation. Regardless, no one in charge seemed to know we were there, so we had the opportunity to create our own agendas.

On the day we arrived, the beautiful 1,800-acre campus on the shores of Lake Maxinkuckee was awash with the activity of nearly 1350 campers and 350 staff members, who clearly had their days fully committed to the skill and habit-building that would transform these young people into leaders and responsible citizens — even the nine-year-olds. The result was that we had our second opportunity to pass relatively unnoticed among those working hard for Culver. It also provided the perfect time to "learn by walking around." Every department was in nearly full operation, since Culver could never operate its summer program without a maintenance department, an active boat crew, staffing for the stables and horsemanship program, a full Food Service staff, a fully operational Laundry and Uniform Department, a bustling Human Resources function, and a Technology Department. These departments and their employees were hard at work, and Pam and I had the best seats in the house to learn about what they did and how they served the Academy.

I recall vividly the first few days we were on campus as the "official" Head of Schools. We arrived during the weekend of the 4th of July celebration; and Culver,

The arresting sight of Culver sailboats adorning the waters of Aubbeenaubbee Bay marks a typical summer day at Culver.

in patriotic fashion, had planned its annual and legendary celebration for the summer schoolers and campers, the faculty and staff, the Town of Culver, and for any people who happened to be driving in for the affair. Unfortunately, we had no idea that it was taking place or that it was a signature ceremony for the Camp. Someone must have missed the memo that the new Head of Schools and his spouse were arriving that weekend.

We were asked to camp out for a few weeks in a guest cottage on the Lake while the School finished preparing the home we would be living in on campus, so we had just settled into this rustic cottage when the fireworks barrage began. We certainly knew we were coming to a military school, but the explosions were something we had not anticipated. Quickly, we put two and two together and realized that this was the 4th and there obviously was a celebration. We headed over to the campus, found an empty boat tied to a pier to sit in, and watched one of the most spectacular fireworks displays we had ever seen. We joked that this was our welcome to Culver, but that the staff was either too shy to tell us about it or wanted it to be a surprise.

The real surprises, however, came early the next morning. We were relaxing over a cup of coffee when we were almost literally blown out of our seats. The small and quaint cottage serving as our temporary quarters literally shook. "What was that?" It sounded and felt as though someone had fired a cannon somewhere. I dressed quickly and headed toward the office to ensure that everything was all right on campus, feeling the responsibility of leadership already. I asked Pam to meet me later that morning for a tour and then lunch in the Dining Hall.

Culver Summer Schools and Camps' flagship vessel the R.H. Ledbetter, the largest three-masted boat on US inland waters.

She arrived a few hours later and was excited to tell me that she had walked to the office by way of the walkway on the lakefront and had two discoveries, both surprising and positive. First, she gasped, "I found what made that noise this morning, and it really was a cannon!" "I know," I said, smiling.

"But the best thing is what I saw on the Lake as I walked over here. The Lake and every other inch of ground is filled with color, activity, and the sounds of children having fun. It looked like a human kaleidoscope of joy." She was absolutely thrilled.

We would continue to see that same phenomenon throughout our first day. We saw young people marching everywhere they went. We saw young people cheering as they marched. We saw young people instructing, leading, and supporting others. At lunch, we learned very quickly and definitively that the building we were having lunch or DRC (Dinner Roll Call) in should be referred to by its proper name — the Mess Hall, not the Dining Hall. Remember that this is a military school, actually a Summer School with a military model of leadership training; and even if it were not, we would respect the traditional names used for these important buildings… so it was the Mess Hall.

Tradition and celebration were obvious everywhere. Kindness and respect were evident in the universal agreement about greeting each other on the sidewalks and fields. Leadership and followership were being practiced all day in every activity. The campus was beautifully attended to, reflecting the pride and attention to detail the staff exhibited in carrying out its responsibilities. Finally, the

Among the colorful and challenging annual mainstays of Culver's summer programs are the Upper Camp Girls' Great Race, above, and the Kline Relay for boys, top.

summer employees spared no effort, personally or professionally, to support these industrious and optimistic young people. After our first day, Pam and I were certain that the promise we had seen inscribed on the Culver Legion Crest above the fireplace in the Alumni Lounge of the Legion Memorial Building was being lived out daily. We had no information about the history of the Crest, but its prominent position above the hearth of this great and historical space suggested its importance. Using my best Latin training, I pieced together the following from the inscription that ringed the assembled symbols:

"Let us learn to use these signs and symbols as our guideposts and goals."

The Crest was decorated with four insignias representing service, justice, wisdom, and friendship — the guideposts and goals. This all seemed perfectly appropriate and totally inspiring to us on Day 1, but it would not be until months later that we learned the history of the Crest and the significance of it for Culver.

The next three weeks passed too quickly. There were Parades for all 1,350 young people every Sunday after mandatory morning Chapel and Mass. They showcased the Summer School Horsemanship students with 50 mounted Troopers; the Naval Band with 60 Upper School musicians, playing drums and their brass and reed instruments; an Aviation Unit with 60 aviators, while four more maneuvered planes above the Parade Field, executing a fly-over; and five boys' Naval Companies and seven girls' Decks, each featuring 60 midshipmen or women. In addition, there were 700 Woodcrafters, divided into the following units: Cubs and Beavers for boys; Butterflies and Cardinals for girls; and their marching band — the Woodcraft Drum and Bugle Corps. Leading the Upper School parade was the Regimental Commander and his or her staff, as well as the Woodcraft Regimental Commander and his or her staff. This was a spectacular display of military discipline and leadership, especially since the entire operation was being led and managed by young leaders, not adults.

The CGA Crest originally served as the Culver Legion's coat of arms, and was adopted as the formal Crest for The Culver Academy for Girls in 1971.

These parades served as evidence for the claims of the Summer Program. Young people learned the skills and attitudes of leadership and responsible citizenship while building their minds and bodies during the six weeks they were in camp and during the nine years total they can be a part of the summer program overall — six in Woodcraft and three in Naval, Aviation, Horsemanship or the Girls' Schools. Parades also provide the parents the opportunity to see what their children have been doing, learning, and achieving. And, yes, achievement is important. There are two significant tasks young people, especially young boys, need to master — competition and collaboration. Both are a challenge for young people, and both are taught and learned by being a part of a formal Parade.

These lessons learned are reinforced further by the regular evening retreat ceremonies, formations for all three meals, and the creation and reinforcement of the habits of leadership and character they engage in throughout the week. Maybe most important, they are learning that a key component of leadership is in the "doing" and in "making something happen." Then when the parade concludes, Woodcraft parents

The Naval Band passes in review during parade.

leave the parade ground to gather at the Woodcraft Camp, where weekly awards are handed out for performance of groups and individuals — the concept being that external rewards translate into internal motivation to replicate right action, always.

Pam and I also had the opportunity to get behind the pomp and circumstance and see the real work of the Summer School. We visited every department and met all the people who made Culver special. Many had been serving Culver for decades and many others had attended the program themselves. There were teachers and administrators on their own summer vacations who believed that a summer at Culver energized them and made them better teachers and people. Then, there were the members of the Winter School staff — teachers and administrators — who loved being a part of this special program and who appreciated the opportunity for their children to attend. All this observation reinforced our initial feelings: Culver was being true to its Mission of preparing its students and campers for leadership and responsible citizenship in society by developing and nurturing the whole individual — mind, character, spirit, and body. We concluded that if Culver Military Academy and the Culver Girls' Academy were as true to the Culver Mission as the Summer Schools and Camps were, all should be well with the Academies, now and in the future. We also had hosted our first meeting of the Board of Trustees in early July, and that meeting gave us the opportunity to connect with our Trustees and to learn more about their engagement with and commitment to their School.

You will recall that we had met many board members during the interviewing process and had been impressed and surprised by the stature of these Culver men and women. Nearly all were personally successful and responsible for both their businesses and the people who worked for them. Furthermore, many of them served their colleges and universities as trustees and were equally active in and supportive of their communities and their important charities. These people were doing well and doing good. Those not leading businesses were leaders in the military, the medical professions, and served as managing partners of law firms or as judges. These were incredibly busy people, yet they traveled to a meeting of their high school's Board of Trustees on a Thursday in Indiana; and they spent most of the weekend attending to the well-being of Culver.

During the vetting process, both Pam and I had begun to share with our children our reaction to the quality of the people on the Culver Board of Trustees. The more board members we met, the more examples we had of the Culver product and brand as embodied in the members of its Trustees. We learned that Board members served on the governing boards (often as Chairs) of Harvard, Yale, Princeton, Chicago, Trinity University, Vanderbilt, Old Dominion, Northwestern, and the University of Texas. They served as CEOs of Cummins Engine, Crown Equipment Corp., Rohm and Haas, Landmark Communications (The Weather Channel), The Tribune Company, and Abbott Labs. Two served individually as the President of AT&T and Texaco. Another was the Managing Partner of Cravath, Swain, & Moore, one of the most recognized and highly respected law firms in the world. Furthermore, those not running major businesses were providing service to society and leading their organizations and communities in important and responsible ways.

I recall telling our daughter, a Harvard and Harvard Business School graduate, how genuine and impressive these people were, and she responded, "It can't be Culver!" But the more people from Culver we met, people who fit this same mold of leadership and service, the more her resolve waivered to "It can't be Culver…can it?" to "Maybe it is Culver." Our son, a Morehead Scholar at the University of North Carolina and a graduate of Princeton's School of Public Policy, seemed intrigued that whereas most of the trustees of his school (our former school) came from the investment banking world and did not ever have to worry about making payroll, i.e., being responsible for others, Culver Trustees

Nature study and scouting-related activities are among the wide array of Culver Summer Schools & Camps offerings.

were truly responsible for their employees. We were beginning to parse out the response we would spend the next 17 years crafting to the question: "Why Culver?" Clearly, these Trustees — all Culver alumni and alumnae — represented the virtues and values that Culver espoused. The next question was whether this standard of integrity and personal success — not just wealth — was being reached by the majority of alumni and, more important, by younger alumni, those who went through the Academy and its schools after the Vietnam War.

Before we knew it, the CMA football team was back for early practice in August. The Summer School had graduated its Upper Schools' First Classmen and Women and its Woodcraft Camp Gold C Beavers and Cardinals; the 80 horses had been put back out into the pasture to gain some weight and rest up after a hot summer; the faculty had returned for their organizational meetings; and we were planning to start our first year of CMA and CGA with a Winter School registration and an Inaugural Convocation Ceremony. This was the start of our real education.

Chapter Six: Culture is the Formative Glue that Holds a School Together

(Thomas J. Sergiovanni)

We should not have been surprised that Culver had a grand plan for welcoming us as its twelfth Superintendent, or in my case, Head of Schools, in spite of our inauspicious entrance only two months earlier. The opening convocation turned out to be a ceremony befitting a college president, possibly because Culver's board chair was also Princeton's board chair, and he had recently installed the new President at Princeton. It was not exactly a coronation, but it was a formal convocation during which both the retiring Superintendent and the Superintendent before him — two men beloved by their School — welcomed Pam and me, spoke wisely and passionately about the importance of the Academy and its mission, and even presented me with a medallion symbolizing the sacred trust I was agreeing to embrace in becoming only the 12th Head of Schools in Culver's history.

John Buxton's Installation Ceremony in August, 1999, with former superintendents Ralph Manuel (1982-99) and John Mars (1976-81) present, to pass the leadership baton.

The entire student body was there in their most formal uniforms and wardrobes — Dress A, as it is called. The faculty and staff processed into the Memorial Chapel in their academic regalia. Dozens of retired faculty and staff were invited, as well as leaders from the Town of Culver. There were also a surprisingly large number of Trustees who had made the trip to witness and support this formal transfer of responsibility. I had been told I would have an opportunity to make my remarks, after I had been formally introduced by Jim Henderson, the Chairman of the Board. I will never forget the solemnity of the evening, the advice and wisdom that was shared, or the celebratory tone of the process. It was Culver's way of telling us that while we had their support, this was an exceedingly important assignment because it was a place that mattered to so many.

Left: New Culver students, during their orientation process, are not only told the story of the Logansport flood rescue of 1913, but also asked to row smaller versions of the cutter boats used in that event, demonstrating to them the importance of teamwork and both followship and leadership.

Jim Henderson's comments that evening were particularly impactful. Once he began, it was clear to me that his message was aimed at the students and the faculty, as well as toward Pam and me. He was welcoming all the new students for whom this event was their first introduction to the mores of Culver. He reminded them skillfully that "you will find that Culver is a place that challenges you and can bring out the best in you, if you are willing." He added beautifully to that challenge by telling them and us that "Culver can also capture your heart for life in the process, and graduates of all ages can attest to that."

He reminded everyone that this year would provide the perfect time to be envisioning our future not only because it was the start of the new Millennium, but also a time to take stock of where we have been as a way of helping inform us about where we are headed. He added that as we review our mission and objectives as a school, we should remember that Culver has always emphasized academic preparation of the highest order as it sought to build the character of the students and to influence their values. Then, he punctuated that statement by saying, "And Culver has always emphasized student leadership — more than any other secondary school I know." I had heard these sentiments and personal commitments before…when we first met in Boston to discuss the position. Now he was framing the conversation and the narrative about Culver with its youngest students and its newest faculty members and staff.

He then proceeded to read Culver's Mission statement:

> "We strive to prepare our students for leadership and responsible
> citizenship in Society by developing and nurturing the whole individual
> — mind, character, spirit, and body."

He finished his remarks, that were primarily directed to the students, by reminding them of the leadership and service that Culver graduates have given to the country in both World Wars and the conflicts that followed them, making sacrifices for which they were honored in the creation of the beautiful and inspiring Chapel in which we were meeting.

Next, he turned to me and said, "John, today the board of trustees of the Culver Educational Foundation officially entrusts this institution to your leadership. We know you have a deep respect for our roots and past accomplishments. We know you have a strong commitment to our statement of mission and objectives. We look forward to your thoughts, ideas, and energy in pursuit of those objectives. We want to be able to measure our success, so we can pursue continuous improvement. We want to be the very best. We believe we can be the very best."

He continued by reminding me that Pam and I already had the support of the faculty, the students, the parents, and of an alumni body that is "uncommon in its love of this institution and its dedication to what we are trying to do here. I know they will support your efforts."

Then he ended by saying that the board of trustees "pledges to you our full support and expresses to you our great joy that you are here. So, it is my pleasure to officially bestow upon you the title of Head of Schools of the Culver Academies."

The storytelling had begun. Jim Henderson had seized this opportunity to galvanize the Culver Academies' community around the Mission and Principles of the Institution and had alerted everyone associated with the Academies that we were all reading from the same sheet of music. His message was that our newly elected Head of Schools, and his wife, were fully briefed and well-versed in the principles of whole person education and understood and accepted its commitment to the development of leadership and character. We could now begin our work together on the "continuous improvement" model that was a given for any serious leader.

In the coming weeks I would "see a great deal by observing." Every member of the community was eager to inform Pam and me about their version of the reality of Culver but having been a party to four other head of school transitions in my career, I understood this phenomenon. Everyone lined up to share with the new Head what needed to be done to change the school for the better. One well-established administrator suggested we evaluate seriously a different leadership model for the boys. Another presented the overworked faculty lobby. I imagine my conversations covered nearly every aspect of the school, and of every school. I understood there was good information in all their agendas, but each request or suggestion was incomplete because it lacked context. I needed to find the ground truth, and I was more interested in seeing the walk — walked — than talked.

As I made my rounds those first 100 days, as it were, I began to understand the context, as well as the specifics, of the system. This would be my version of a formal S.W.O.T. (Strengths, Weaknesses, Opportunities, and Threats) analysis and an exercise in management by walking around. My method would be to become fully a part of the Academy. Pam and I would eat in the Mess Hall, visit classes — all of them, literally — drop in on athletic practices, meet with faculty and employee departments and "stand B.I.," as the Barrack Inspector, the adult in charge.

After six months of study about Culver and the military model of leadership, and after having had two months of Summer Schools and Camps' experience, I was beginning to formulate my own sense of the way things were. I made notes on my observations from the first six months, and I was mostly optimistic about what I saw. The highlight was the performance of my Unit duty Officer during Barracks Inspection. I saw evidence that students could provide guidance and an example for their younger counterparts. That duty as a B.I. showed me that today's Culver was as serious about accountability and personal responsibility as the institution had ever been historically. However, there was another experience that, while hopeful, suggested that not everyone understood Culver equally well.

The process in CMA is called "Boards." The new cadets spend the first six months of the year (it used to be a full year) learning

One of Culver's seminal daily rituals is the solemn, ceremonial lowering of the flag by cadets each evening at retreat.

about the Culver Military Cadet System before being interviewed and then vetted for their being welcomed officially into the Corps of Cadets. They have to learn the history of Culver, the technical skills of the Battalion with which each is associated: Artillery (the Batteries), Infantry (the Companies), and the Squadron (Troops and Band), the Code of Conduct and the CMA Cadet Creed. They also are being evaluated on their performance during the New Cadet program. For instance, how well did they learn to take care of themselves — policing their rooms, attending to their appearance and hygiene, meeting their academic commitments, contributing to the well-being of the Unit competitions, and participating in close-order drill. They have been practicing and drilling, marching in parades, doing chores in the Unit, and learning from the example and direction of the older cadets, their leaders; and in every action they have been observed and evaluated for their readiness to be a member of the Corps.

Commandant Col. Al Shine, US Army Ret. (who served in that role from 1990 to 2000), in conversation with John and Pam Buxton after a Sunday parade.

The Commandant (the chief adult administrator for CMA and for all intents and purposes, the Dean of Boys) had invited me to sit in on a part of the Boards process and to see this rite of passage up close and personal. I was more than intrigued; I was thrilled to see our leadership training program in action. I would learn so much by understanding what the student leaders valued enough to include in the interview part of the process. I had not been in the room as the new cadets completed their skill tests in music or their horsemanship skills testing in the indoor riding arena. I was there, however, for this interview. The cadet officers who made up the interview committee were dressed in formal Dress A and were serious in their approach and demeanor. They quizzed the new cadet seated in front of them in rapid fire fashion, but they were not dismissive or unsupportive. This was a serious process, because for the system to work, people had to take it seriously.

After the questions about the Superintendents of the Academies — who they were and when they served — the leaders asked each new cadet to explain the significance of two of the great Culver stories: The Big Fire and the Logansport Flood. I had read about both in Bob Hartman's book, and I had actually spent time trying to see the value in each as a "guidepost or goal." The new cadets answered the questions fairly accurately, but they did not truly have the vocabulary or the conceptual understanding to answer them contextually. One boy said that the moral of the 1900 Big Fire story, in which 105 cadets were expelled for supporting two popular cadets who had been dismissed, was that the cadets who were expelled for supporting their friends had shown loyalty and courage in deciding to ignore the wishes and orders of the Administration. This was not the takeaway I had expected or hoped for, but they were responding as adolescents normally would. Fortunately, they had the Logansport Flood story down pretty well, but once again, they did not as a group possess a common language to discuss the virtues and values being displayed in this heroic rescue. This was an important piece of the puzzle for me. I also saw it as both a challenge and an opportunity.

Culver's iconic narratives are supposed to amplify what the Academy values, what it believes, and what its purpose is. The Big Fire story framed for me the definition of personal responsibility and accountability, and it delineated the difference between duty and honor. To refresh your memory — if you are a graduate — a cadet and his friend went to Town at the time that Town privileges were not permitted liberally. As a result, both were dismissed from the Academy and were directed to take the train home. Distraught that their friends were leaving, the other cadets assembled on campus to accompany them to the train station in town to see them off as they departed. The Commandant, Maj. Gignilliat, called all of the boys — who represented at least two thirds of the Academy's student population — together and explained to them that they, too, would be guilty of the same transgression if they walked into town to say goodbye. The students did not heed the warning and all were expelled. No one could believe that Culver would stand on principle in the extreme, but the leadership of the Academy believed that this would be an important lesson for the boys. All but a few returned, some within a few days and others within a few weeks, but the point had been made. This may have been about justice and courage, but ironically, both sides were demonstrating these same virtues. What the students needed to learn was how difficult it is to separate duty from honor, as well as what it means to be personally responsible for one's decisions. They also needed to understand the virtues of wisdom and moderation.

The Logansport, Indiana flood story provides more inspiration, but it was equally instructional for the cadets. Furthermore, the moral is incredibly important for understanding the value proposition for Culver. You can be assured that this narrative will never be a case study for responsible risk management. The winter storms and flooding in the Midwest in March of 1913 were biblical, and the National Guardsmen were stretched thin. Rivers were overflowing their banks and dams and levees were being compromised. The call from Logansport, which sits at the junction of two rivers — the Wabash and the Eel — came late in the evening to Maj. Gignilliat at his home on campus. The mayor of Logansport was calling to ask that the Academy allow Logansport to borrow the Academy's 12-oared "crew" boats to be used to rescue many of their citizens from the roofs of their homes, having been stranded there by the raging waters of the flood.

Gignilliat consulted E.R. Culver, head of Culver's board of trustees, and his commandant — Col. Robert Rossow — and made the decision to send not only the boats but as many boys as would be needed to man the crafts during the rescue, if necessary. Sending dozens of young men into the teeth of a terrifying flood may not have been the obvious decision for a Head of School to

Cutter number 13 symbolized Culver's remarkable service and duty in rescuing Logansport citizens.

Landing passengers by transfer from Cutter to Navy boat of lighter draft after water had fallen Thursday

For 36 straight hours in March, 1913, Culver cadets in cutters rescued some 1,500 Logansport, Ind. citizens from a devastating flood.

A Culver cadet alongside the newly-dedicated Logansport Gate, in 1914.

make in a situation like this, but the urgency of the matter and the confidence the Academy's leaders had in their cadets made it more understandable. Gignilliat did not send the boys knowing they would be responsible for the rescue; but he certainly must have known that it was a possibility. Regardless, he packed the boys and boats on the train to Logansport in the middle of the night in the rain, sleet, and snow in an effort to do the right thing by providing both leadership and service to people in desperate trouble. The story ends well, with all the more than 1,492 stranded citizens of Logansport safely rescued and no casualties noted. The crews of cadets completed their work after 36 hours of effort and personal sacrifice — fueled mostly by hot coffee. Once the rescue was complete, the boys marched back to the train station, singing as they went. One newspaper account described the response of the Academy by explaining that the citizens of Logansport were feeling hopeless until they saw "them boys from Culver" coming to the rescue. That gave them hope (note: one night while attending an engagement with a few people from the town of Culver and their friends from the area, I was introduced to a man who had grown up in Logansport, so I asked him if he was familiar with the story of the flood. He explained excitedly that his great-grandmother was one of the toddlers rescued from a rooftop, and if not for the Culver cadets, he would not have been standing there that evening. I felt chills).

How is it possible that these approximately five dozen young men had the wherewithal to pull off such a heroic feat? Training, resilience, and character. The "crew" boats they used in the rescue were 22 feet long and weighed nearly a ton. They had a rudder that had to be manned for steering, and they carried 12 oars. You could not take just any 14 boys from a group and ask them to do what the Culver boys did that day and a half. Most of the boys chosen to participate from the Winter School cadet corps had at some point been part of the Summer Naval School program and had been trained in the use of these boats, with the remainder selected from the ranks of Culver's football team: big, strong, eager young men who would learn what to do quickly and would also have the resolve to complete the task. They had the qualities outlined in the Spirit of Culver: "the hope to win and the zeal to dare." They were Culver men; no one should have been surprised.

There is one footnote that I found particularly interesting and ironic, and it relates to the difficulty of explaining Culver to outsiders. The Academy had made the decision to create a summer experience as a way of generating interest in the Winter School, and in 1902 proudly announced the opening of its Summer Naval School on the shores of Lake Maxinkuckee. Ironically, one source of negative response to the opening was the Logansport *Chronicle* newspaper, which suggested that Culver's ties to the U.S. Navy were exaggerated. Yet 11 years later, the city understood the power of preparation at Culver and its well-trained midshipmen.

As you can see, I was learning daily the answers to the question: Why Culver? Soon into my first year, I was presented with a copy of a piece that had been commissioned by one of the best marketing and sales people of all time — Joe Levy, an entrepreneur, a collector, and most important of all, a mentor to those who needed him. Joe graduated from Culver in 1943 and was in the Artillery Battalion. At that time, the Artillery — the unit that fires the cannons — was horse-drawn and not a mechanized unit. The cadets in the Artillery had to saddle and hitch up teams of horses to pull the caissons to the battlefields. At Culver there were no battlefields, but there were drills and parades, and the boys had to be fully trained to be able to handle their responsibilities with the horses and cannons, just as the Naval Schoolers were with the crew boats.

Joe was a "doer," a man of action and results. At one point in his career he had been the world's largest Buick dealer by volume. His dealership in Chicago was legendary, and it may be the reason so many people sought him out for advice and guidance. It also meant that when Joe identified an opportunity or a problem, he pursued it doggedly. He decided, therefore, to address the issue of Culver's relative obscurity and determined that Culver's virtual Who's Who of graduates was a selling point and a place to start. He published a small leaflet entitled, "Why Culver?" in which he featured the most successful alumni from six different decades/vintages as proof of the power and importance of Culver.

The book was widely circulated among alumni, but its outreach was ultimately limited because it was an in-house document, as it were. People who had already heard the stories about Culver being CEO-central were the ones receiving the information. It was a closed loop. Still, the pamphlet inspired others to imagine a way to

Culver's horse-drawn artillery passing in review circa 1930s-40s.

get the story of the Academy understood by a wider audience. How about a piece in the *Wall Street Journal* or the *New York Times*? Some suggested a book written by a professional writer on the magic, or the specialness, or the uniqueness of Culver. The hue and cry from the alumni was uniform — we need to be better known.

Halfway through our first year, we had a Board meeting in Dallas. Our practice as a Board was moving the winter planning meeting around the country each year to stay in contact with alumni near and far. At one of the luncheons for alumni and school families in Dallas, I made a comment I would quickly come to regret. I opined that Culver had to be one of the "best kept secrets in America." After the event a retired faculty member living in the Dallas area approached me and cautioned me that one of the most controversial and shortest-serving Superintendents ever at Culver had used exactly those words in one of his first addresses, and the retiree thought I should be forewarned that such an approach did not turn out well for him. Back to the drawing board.

The answer began to come to me, and the best indicator had been not so subtly embedded in Jim Henderson's charge to me in the Opening Convocation: We must find a way to measure what we do — to measure our success. If one cannot measure the value proposition, the success, or the quality of its programs, why should anyone take the claimant —us and our alumni — seriously? We needed not only aspirational symbols; we needed data to serve as warrants for our claims.

We also had to prove relevance, taking us back to the buggy whip analogy. Building the best buggy whip mattered in the late 19th century, but once cars were being manufactured regularly, buggies became an artifact of the past. We had to demonstrate that Culver still mattered, and not only had a seat at the table for the conversation about education, but also was a leader in the debate and a shining example of best practices and best outcomes. We had to do more than proclaim our own success based upon what we considered an impressive array of successful graduates.

CHAPTER SEVEN: A COMMITMENT TO SERVICE AND LEADERSHIP

Isolation can be lonely...and misleading. Yogi Berra didn't say this, but he might have. After all, there are many things Yogi said that he assures us he never said — "I didn't really say all of the things I said!" Early on in our career at Culver, I had an opportunity to have lunch in the Mess Hall with a few graduates from the 1970s. They were regaling me with their version of the challenges Culver faced in the decade of the '70s dealing with the image of the military, integrating the Academy racially, and coping with the social revolution and "drugs, sex, and rock and roll." As they outlined for me all of Culver's challenges, it occurred to me that they were describing quite well the exact experiences I had lived through in our well-financed, uncomplicated, and rather typical eastern boarding school during that same period. What surprised me was their sense that all of this had happened because they were a military school. Their assessment of the situation was that I probably could not relate to their experiences because our school had not been a military school. When I explained to them that our school back east had had exactly those issues, they were completely surprised. All this time they believed that the intensity of their version of these problems had been exacerbated by their military school culture. Their challenge was finding context. They were not situated near any other similar schools, so it was understandable that they assumed their challenges in these arenas were theirs alone.

I began to realize that Culver needed to see itself in the context of other successful "leadership" schools. There were so many important programs at Culver that had been an integral part of its history, and either the Academy had come to take them for granted or it did not realize how special these programs were. I recall telling the Chairman of the Board that for almost all the years we had been at our former school — arguably considered one of the top three in the country — we had been twisting ourselves around our own axle trying to figure out how to create a successful, student leadership training program — reference the Unit Duty Officer story. Culver needed to focus on what it stood for, what it was achieving, and what it had accomplished that mattered in today's world.

Once again, I found myself wishing I had had these insights and this knowledge — or at least, this information — as I was putting together my graduate school course of study of Culver's challenge in the 21st century. I reflected on the process I had been going through in my graduate program and realized that all I had accomplished was gathering some of the puzzle pieces on the card table and managed to place only the corner pieces where they belonged. Now, after six months, I was beginning to see definite patterns emerging, and they were coming together to create a puzzle picture that reflected clearly what I had been hearing from Culver's staunchest supporters, at least, conceptually. Just as the new cadets did not have the language to express

Emily Jane Hand Culver and Henry Harrison Culver, the Academy's founding couple.

fully and clearly what they were trying to describe during the Boards process, these loyal alumni were simply missing the right vocabulary. After all, who has the time or the inclination to engage in an academic assessment of their high school's philosophy? Wasn't it enough to cherish and support the place that had made all the difference in your life and had prepared you for the future…your future?

By this time, I had the background to understand fully how Culver had come into being as the school we happened upon. The Culver family had the vision to build a school for boys on a pristine and inspirational piece of land in the middle of the territory where the family business sold its product — Wrought Iron Range Stoves. As they had built a business, they had also built a school, and while they were fully invested in the project, they were wise enough to allow professional educators to advise them. Remember, Henry Harrison Culver — the man with the dream and the vision — had been the beneficiary of only a limited education. This may not have been unusual for a young man growing up in the late 1800s before the Civil War, but his lack of formal education may have been a driving force in his determination to provide the opportunity for the young men who would be served by this new school — Culver Academy. His muse, as it were, in the process of founding a school was his wife, Emily Jane Hand Culver, a young woman from nearby Wolf Creek. She was formally educated and an inspiration to him. She understood far more about the principles of schooling, and she undoubtedly helped frame his early ideas about what he wanted to accomplish for his students.

The product from St. Louis that made the creation of H.H. Culver's "Castle in the Air," Culver Military Academy, possible: the Home Comfort, or Wrought Iron Range, stove.

Yet, his first important hire — his first Superintendent, Reverend John H. McKenzie — came to Culver from a Church school that used a military model of education, so he believed there was good reason for embracing this approach. Unfortunately, he believed that the school should be called St. Paul's School and not Culver Academy. These ill-timed and poorly conceived recommendations led to Culver's first Superintendent being relieved of his duty. However, this early disappointment may have been fortuitous for Culver. After an interim appointment of a U.S. Army officer, Major Clinton Tebbetts, the way was opened for a truly important recruitment process, masterminded by H.H. Culver himself: the hiring of Col. Alexander Fleet. Having served in the Civil War, Fleet was serving as the Superintendent of Missouri Military Academy when that

The remains of Missouri Military Academy's campus after the 1896 fire that brought Col. Fleet, his administrators, and many of his cadets, to Culver.

school had a fire that literally destroyed all the Academy's school buildings. Word of the fire reached H.H. Culver, who immediately sent a telegram to Col. Fleet explaining that "We've got the buildings, and you've got the boys. Let's get together." The rest, as they say, is history.

Col. Fleet's arrival was significant for so many reasons. First, he brought with him useful experience in running a military academy, a deep knowledge of the classical, Aristotelian model of education; an awareness and acceptance of the citizen-soldier concept; a deeply engraved character, and two of Missouri Military Institute's top administrators, one of whom would become the headmaster

Assembled at Culver is the new leadership team as photographed in 1896, including Col. Alexander Fleet (top center), Lt. L.R. Gignilliat (at Fleet's immediate right), and Cols. Glascock and Greiner (at Fleet's left). Also pictured are faculty members Stewart, Jaeger, Lewin, and McIntyre.

and the other the Commandant. Fleet, as it turned out, made a critically important hire in 1897 when he picked Major Leigh Gignilliat from Virginia Military Institute to serve as his commandant. Gignilliat was barely old enough to grow a moustache when he was hired, but he went on to distinguish himself as a leader in World War I, a strong Commandant, and a great visionary and leader as Superintendent of Culver Military Academy. He also was the perfect son-in-law for the Fleets after he fell in love with and married their daughter, Mary.

When it had first been established, Culver was a proprietary institution, owned and operated by the Culver family. The Culvers built the buildings from the proceeds of their businesses, and when times were tough, the family simply halted or postponed the building projects on the campus until the economy sorted things out. Then in 1932, having survived the Great Depression and all the financial ramifications that accompanied it, the Culver family made a most special gift to its alumni, while also handing over the greatest responsibility it had: the ownership of the Academy. The Culver Covenant signified the gifting of the Academy to the alumni of the school. The Culver family had conceived of, built, and sacrificed personally to finance the Academy. Now it was ready to gift what it had built to its extended family — its graduates.

Although 1932 marked the beginning of the Culver alumni's taking over the ownership of the Academy, it would not be for several years that Culver would set up a formal fundraising operation and begin to ask alumni to support their school financially (this began during World War II when fundraising began for the Memorial Chapel). In fact, General Gignilliat was on record as not wanting the alumni to feel the pressure of financing Culver. He felt strongly that Culver Military Academy was providing a public service by educating the next generation of civic leaders or, if the world was headed in the direction of another world war, the next generation of military service-men and leaders. He had taken seriously the "moral equivalent of war" analogy that the educational philosopher, William James, had made at the turn of the century. American education was focused on building…its responsibility was to build both things and people. In fact, the early Culver Alumni magazine was referred to as "The Builder." In an early publication of an admissions brochure entitled "Men in the Making," the Culver Fathers' Association, created by Col. John Henderson, published the following: "Some of our Culver graduates are in universities, some are out in the World. They're building bridges, writing novels. They are doctors and lawyers, and junior captains of industry." The American experience, and the Culver experience, were about building a world out of the frontier, not unlike building a business from a concept or a school from an idea, and then persisting and prevailing, having the courage to realize the vision.

Cover of the *Culver Alumnus* magazine from November, 1977.

Culver decided early on in its life as an institution that education was a service, an opportunity to educate the young men in its care so they would be prepared to protect and serve the "common weal." Whatever Culver taught had to be for the service of the democracy, so its educational principles had to be about both knowledge and action, and both of those outcomes had to be informed by right action, always. It did not depend only on the military principles and the skills its leaders had learned in battles; it reached out to the experts in the field of education to educate itself on the best practices at the highest levels of the educational hierarchy to ensure it was making the best decisions for the Academy and for the future of its students.

In the 1930s Culver contacted Harvard University, the University of Wisconsin, and the University of Michigan and invited their most distinguished advisers to consult with Culver about its educational philosophy and practices. Culver leaders requested a thorough appraisal of Culver's program "in light of recognized changes in educational practices nationally, new trends in national life (after World War I and the Great Depression); and the purpose of providing, as nearly as possible, the ideal education for the American preparatory school boy." Culver examined critically its whole scheme of training — scholastic, military, and athletic — and said to itself, "How can we best coordinate the whole school program to give the student what he must get in adolescence for useful, happy living?" Culver was open to a process of self-reflection and evaluation from outside advisers to validate its best thinking and planning for CMA. Even at this early juncture, Culver was clear about what it wanted for its students and was willing to make the necessary adjustments, regardless of its history and special legacy, to do the right thing for its students and for the country.

These distinguished advisers made a series of recommendations to the leadership at Culver, but for the most part, they encouraged Culver to retain its practical education approach to its curriculum. Not all graduates from even the most prestigious private high schools were destined for college. In fact, college was a luxury of sorts, reserved mainly for those who could afford it and those not fully ready to enter the world of business. Many schools like Culver were still offering training in business practices, in addition to an introduction to a classical educational track. Culver determined that its emphasis on both the military and useful training for the future made sense, given its history, its mission, and its clientele. This proved to be a most important decision for the Academy and one it would never regret.

All this information about Culver's approach to building the best educational model was a part of its history, but it was not readily available to those attending the Academy. Culver wanted to determine what young people needed and then build out the model that would ensure the desired result. Culver's leaders also understood that there was a Second World War on the horizon, and though the country was not certain America would have a part in it, it was certainly possible that Americans might be asked to engage. If this were to happen, Culver wanted to be certain that its graduates were prepared. When the Mexican-American Border Wars were breaking out on the south-western borders of the United States before World War I, and Pancho Villa's army needed to be engaged militarily, Culver was authorized by the U.S. military to set up student-led training camps on its campus to prepare both high school youth from around Indiana, as well as its own alumni, to get into the fray.

This endeavor, one of many from that period which helped put Culver on the national map in regard to the war effort, also led to a name change for the school's alumni organization from the lengthy "Culver Military Academy Alumni Association" to simply, "the Culver Legion," as it has stood ever since.

Culver's little "Legion" of men were getting ready to head west when the call came for America's participation in WWI, and Culver's "legion" of soldiers headed off to war. The casualties they suffered were significant — Culver's first Gold Star men — 86 in all — represented a significant percentage of the Academy's graduates. Their bravery, courage, and service provided a standard of commitment that would serve Culver as an example of leadership for the next century: Readiness is all. Fit for the Future. The Making of Men. These were the signs and symbols of the "Legion's" Crest.

As Culver weathered the storms of World War II, the Academy grew in reputation and stature. Many of its own graduates and faculty and staff distinguished themselves

Left: An early image of then-Lt. Gignilliat inspecting cadet quarters. Right: Cadets engaged in a bridge building exercise, typical of Gignilliat's vision of youth preparedness, and one indication of why Culver had earned a national reputation for its training capacity by the time World War I was underway.

as leaders and heroes in the War effort, and those too young to serve, learned by their example. This generation — the members of the Greatest Generation whom Pam and I had met during our "meet and greet" luncheons — were vintage Culver. They grew up in a world that understood the value of service. Their fathers and grandfathers had fought for their country. They saw service as a responsibility, if not as a privilege. But they were also coming through the Culver educational prism when preparation for the finest colleges and universities in the world was as important as preparing for war — since it was unlikely there would be another great war in their lifetimes.

These were the halcyon years of Culver. In the three decades from the late 1930s through the mid-1960s, Culver found its stride. It understood the importance of building the foundation of a man, along the lines that the legendary coach, John Wooden, cited when he spoke of his formula for success: strength mentally, industriousness, and loyalty. This, it seems, was the American formula when the members of the greatest generation were growing up. One used the military to provide opportunities for hard work, personal responsibility, teamwork, and loyalty — to oneself and to those dependent on you — this was their Culver experience.

Culver's graduates were trained to thrive in any situation, academic or military. The graduates from these years distinguished themselves as soldiers, leaders in business, and public servants. Admissions numbers grew as did the Academy's national reputation. The aforementioned *Life* and *Time* magazine articles portrayed Culver for its successful and laudatory combination of academic and personal excellence. Culver was riding the wave of popularity and esteem.

It is no wonder that those who were now providing leadership and guidance for the Academies — the Board of Trustees, most of whom were alumni from these three decades — were deeply concerned about the lack of alignment they saw between their beloved school and an institution struggling to find its place in a changing world and beset by so many challenges: integration, finances, declining enrollment numbers, Vietnam and the loss of faith in America's most cherished institutions, and the social/sexual revolution. Certainly, Culver was not alone, as I pointed out earlier in this chapter, but Culver had an additional burden that only the "church" schools could also claim as an excuse for modest success…it was operating a system that required its students to accept a set of values and participate in a program that was extraneous to the regular academic and extracurricular activities of the normal boarding school. Furthermore, if being required to attend Chapel daily at a church school was considered an imposition to students who had come to see the world in more secular terms, being required to march to meals, police their rooms regularly, engage in military drill, and march to a compulsory chapel service on Sundays seemed to be completely unreasonable.

There was no comparable situation in education. But for the church schools and the military schools, each was simply staying true to their mission and operating principles. Church schools believed that if they were going to teach service to others, their students needed time to reflect on their Christian traditions and to learn the lessons of piety and prayer. Most military schools, likewise, were committed to teaching the habits of leadership and responsible citizenship. They were committed to developing young men of character, and they believed that to achieve these outcomes, one needed a formal system to build those habits. You form lifelong habits by repeating tasks and by reinforcing appropriate actions and reactions…until they become who and what you are.

Many years later, David Brooks, the popular and thoughtful social philosopher, authored a book on character entitled "The Social Animal." He explained the development of character as follows:

> "Not one crucial moment shapes a character. Character emerges gradually out of the mysterious interplay of millions of little influences. [There is the] power of community to shape character…the power of small and repetitive action to rewire the fundamental mechanisms of the brain. Small habits and proper etiquette reinforce certain positive ways of seeing the world."

Brooks was describing how complex a process the formation of character really is. In the world of Culver, character is formed by learning to take care of your personal responsibilities, like cleaning your room every morning, making your bed, and "forming up" in ranks for breakfast if you are a cadet, and if you are a member of CGA, by making your bed and cleaning your room daily, and by making the long trek from your dormitory — the girls do not live in barracks and nearly half lived in "the far dorms" — to the Dining Hall, even in the snow, sleet, and rain. Character comes from repetition of those sometimes tedious or unpleasant tasks that form who you are, things you'd rather not have to do, but also things that will teach you resilience, persistence, and responsibility.

Brooks went on to explain in his next book, "The Road to Character," that exemplars, those who taught and guided you by deed and, especially, by example, played a critical role in demonstrating to you what right action, personal responsibility, and kindness looked like, lived out. He labeled the process "moral improvement." The process begins when "the heart is warmed, when we come into contact with people we admire, and we consciously and unconsciously bend our lives to mimic theirs." The Culver story is filled with these models of decorum and care who in the "totality of their life, of the way they go about it in the smallest details, is what gets transmitted."

These exemplars were on the Culver faculty and staff, but they were also in the Cadet Corps' leadership and later in Culver Girls' Academy prefect system's leadership ranks. These were the people who had embraced the Mission and Code of Conduct of Culver as "goals and guideposts" for their own lives. They literally walked the talk of character and leadership. They were the servant leaders who, in seeking to lead, sought first to serve.

Culver's educational philosophy clearly was born from a moral philosophy linked with a practical reality and a world context that cohered to make it all make sense. Maybe Culver was the product of a perfect storm of world events, a country's people embracing America's response to those events, the educational philosophy of the time, and the personal strengths and character of two of its first four leaders — Col. Alexander Fleet and Gen. Leigh Gignilliat. Whatever it was, Culver determined that what young men needed was intellectual health, physical health, and moral health, presented to them in a system that included accountability and personal responsibility. Remember, when considering the context of the time Culver was developing into the school it would become, families were coping with the new challenges of the Industrial Revolution, and families were looking for alternatives to the temptations of the cities for their sons. Boarding schools grew up across the country — but mostly in the East — as a means of removing the sons of the well-to-do from the luxury and ease of home and the temptation of the unhealthy behaviors of city life. These parents were looking for boarding schools off the beaten path that offered them more spartan environments where they could learn the lessons of character on hard bunks and in cold showers, conditions that they were certainly not provided at home.

This was undoubtedly a great school with a significant past and a history of doing exactly the right things educationally. Culver's graduates appreciated what the Academy had done for them, but like so many others, most did not have the language or the information about what was happening currently at the school to be able to synthesize its elements into a single, compelling, and coherent explanation of the mission and program.

CHAPTER EIGHT: SYMBOLS AND CEREMONIES ARE STATEMENTS OF ONE'S VALUES

It appears that Culver may have had a better opportunity carrying this ideal forward into succeeding generations of students than the eastern schools. The warrants that allow me to make this claim are two important traditions in the American experience: the roll calls of a school's history of service in the World Wars, often acknowledged or read aloud during the Veterans' Day and Memorial Day remembrances. I do not have any memory of a Veterans' Day ceremony at our first school, and I believe The Memorial Day service was voluntary, though I recall faculty were encouraged to attend. The headmaster read the Gettysburg Address, shared a few inspirational words, and proceeded to read the list of the names of those graduates who lost their lives in battle. I had been surprised when I compared the number of names of those who lost their lives in World War II, for instance, and how many fewer had died during the Vietnam War or any subsequent military conflicts. It seemed to me that the count dwindled to almost nothing after the first two World Wars. Since I had had no other school to compare it to, I never spent much time thinking about it. Then we arrived at Culver.

As we were moving through our first fall term, we began to hear rumblings about the upcoming Veterans' Day service. I asked what it was exactly and when it would be taking place this year. People looked at me in disbelief. It is the annual ceremony at which we remember all of those who served our country in the military: and it occurs at 11/11/11, at the eleventh hour of the eleventh day of the eleventh month — the date and time the Armistice Treaty was signed, of course. Now, I remembered Armistice Day from my childhood. After all, my great-grandfather, great uncle, grandfather, father, uncle, and brother had all served in the military and all had fought for our country. But I had not celebrated a Veterans' Day that I could remember, as an adult or in a school. I was frankly embarrassed at my lack of knowledge, especially now that we were leading Culver.

The Academy would be conducting the ceremony on Pershing Walk, which was dedicated to General John Pershing after his visit to Culver at the end of World War I. We would be celebrating our veterans in the shadow of the Legion Memorial Building, the building built for and dedicated to those original Gold Star men who had sacrificed their lives in pursuit of our country's liberty and freedom. We would be standing at the hallowed entrance of the building that bore the emblems of the five branches of

Left: Flowers and white dresses were chosen by CGA founding dean Mary Frances England as signature aspects of commencement exercises, from the beginning of the girls' school. The tradition of throwing them aloft at the conclusion of the event is a more recent parallel to the tossing of cadets' garrison caps at the same time.

The Legion Memorial Building, an iconic and symbolic building for Culver alumni and the setting for the Veterans' Day ceremonies.

Capt. Mike Kehoe, US Navy Ret., Commandant of Cadets, addressing CMA cadets and the ladies of CGA during the 2000 Veterans' Day ceremony.

the military — the U.S. Army, U.S. Navy, Marines, U.S. Air Force, and U.S. Coast Guard. There was not a more symbolic building on Culver's campus, with the possible exception of the Memorial Chapel, also a memorial to those Culver graduates who lost their lives in all the wars that followed World War I. This Legion Memorial Building served as the "homestead" — replete with the Gold Star symbols — for all members of the Culver alumni body; it was the place where we celebrated and remembered their service every November.

This was tradition and a part of the Culver experience of every student at Culver — CMA cadets and CGA girls — and had been celebrated for over 80 years by the time Pam and I arrived. This was a compulsory service for all students, faculty, staff and even members of the local community, especially the veterans, were invited to be a part of it.

The speaker for one of the first Veterans' Day Ceremonies we attended was U.S. Navy Capt. Michael Kehoe, who had just begun his tenure as commandant at Culver. His words were perfectly chosen. Not only had he framed the importance of the service, but he had also reminded everyone in attendance of the importance of this tradition. His words reminded me of the words of the Gettysburg Address I recalled from what was a very different ceremony back East, and I wondered what Culver knew or valued that our former school did not. To bring the contrast into even sharper contrast, a few years later I received a call from the mother of a recent graduate of Culver who had discovered that her college did not celebrate Veterans' Day. The young alumna's response, her mother reported proudly, was to request an appointment with the President of the College to discuss why the College did not recognize our veterans on Veterans' Day and to understand what she would need to do to ensure that the college would have such a service going forward. I could not have been more proud, and within a few more years I learned that this young alumna was not alone in making such a request of her university.

Later that first year, we learned that Culver's Memorial Day Service was also very different from the event we had experienced at our former school, memorializing those graduates who died in the "service of their Country." Instead of a somewhat ad hoc gathering of those interested in attending, the Culver ceremony was a gathering of the entire Academy community. We had a visiting speaker whose responsibility and honor it was to put this ceremony into its proper context and who later would preside over the parade in honor of those fallen soldiers we were remembering…"absent but accounted for." Inside the Memorial Chapel where the service was conducted, CMA and CGA leaders were responsible for reading the names of each of the graduates lost to the wars and then presenting wreaths which were then hung on the Gold Star flags, special flags designated for each of the Wars. Afterward, there was a parade in honor of these "heroes of Culver," a 21-gun salute conducted by the Four Gun Drill, the honor unit of the Artillery Battalion, and a Pass in Review of the Culver regiment witnessed by the entire community.

The 2000 Veterans' Day ceremony attended by CMA cadets and CGA students.

Culver wanted to ensure that both its Memorial Day Service and its Veterans' Day Ceremony communicated to its faculty and students that the Academy valued the importance of service in the protection of the freedoms we enjoy today. Culver wanted its students to understand that the Academy's history was steeped in stories of service and sacrifice, and that while in the first seven decades of its history it supported the "War effort," along with many others, Culver continued to provide service to its country, while many other similar schools' students had seemingly opted out. I recall being surprised and impressed that Culver had so many graduates actively involved in fighting the "War on Global Terror" at the beginning of the 21st Century. Culver was proud of its service and the service of its graduates. As someone who had been a witness to military service in my own family, I found the openness and pride in service and in serving our country both refreshing and responsible.

Culver had a belief that while the military training model also worked well for the education of boys and young men, it was not the preparation for war that made it appropriate. Culver believed that learning to be responsible for self, then to be responsible for other duties, then responsible for others, and finally to be responsible for the entire system, developed both one's sense of accountability and personal responsibility. One could not do this unless the training felt real, so there had to be a system in place that afforded young men the opportunity to experience the responsibility of real work, to understand what it meant to be able to take care of your personal duties as a member of a group, to work your way up a ladder of responsibility by achieving what you set out to do and that for which you were accountable. There needed to be a system of graduated privileges that you earned, and there had to be opportunities for you to lead others and be accountable for their well-being. All this came back full circle to H.H. Culver's demand that if Culver were going to become a military school, it had

A CGA student hangs a memorial wreath on Culver's Gold Star flag during the annual Memorial Day Gold Star Ceremony in the Memorial Chapel.

to be predicated on a military model that was of Culver's own design, not the military model used by Norwich University or the Service Academies. His boys were not being trained as soldiers and warriors; rather they were being trained as citizen soldiers, protectors and builders of the Republic.

I imagine that the war in Vietnam and all the controversy, misinformation, disinformation, lack of honesty or transparency, brutality, and shame that became associated with it represented a proverbial fork in the road for America and, by extension, for its schools, especially on the subject of the military. Massacres, loss of civilian life, and mendacity all became entangled in an unfortunate scenario about the brutality and the immorality of war. Everyone even tangentially involved or familiar with war understood that the Vietnam War represented a very different experience than the "Greatest Generation" experienced in World War II. Even then, as brutal and distasteful as the reality of war was, there was a certain honor associated with it. There were reasons to fight the war that were honorable and widely embraced. Our future was at stake, and our soldiers were going across the seas to fight to protect our democratic freedoms. They were welcomed home as heroes then; their service was a demonstration of their loyalty and willingness to sacrifice for the common good.

Consequently, for those at Culver in the 1930s and 1940s, there was no reason not to use their training capabilities to prepare their students for a War (World War II) that seemed both inevitable and justifiable. There was, however, much room for debate about whether the context that emerged in the second half of the Vietnam War merited the same response from a society that viewed this war as abhorrent and emblematic of the duplicity and inhumanity of the military industrial complex. The Vietnam War certainly was not a duty they envisioned as meaningful for their children. The challenge during the 1970s, for Culver and all other military schools, was not only the issue of school finances and declining private school enrollments that we have discussed. They were also fighting the issues highlighted daily in America's newspapers, decrying the horrors and immorality of the military experience of the day.

The only answer for military schools was to either find a different model — which many tried — or to stay the course and hope that the families whose children were potential applicants could understand the power of Plato's model of the citizen/soldier. The challenge was that many of these schools were one-trick ponies. They understood the boot camp drill and training routine better than the academic/citizenship philosophy of AP courses, competitive SAT's and ACT's, and cutting-edge curriculum on the one hand, and meaningful and purposeful drill on the other. The best military secondary schools used the military as a means to an end for training for and teaching about leadership. Their military drill was never about training young men to be combat soldiers. It was a means to teach collaboration, cooperation, and teamwork, as well as attention to detail and accountability.

Unfortunately, many military schools either did not believe they could change gears and transform their models to combinations of high level academic/military training models, or they did not have the financial stability to take on such an investment; so these military schools stuck loyally to the tried and true ROTC model: they hired veterans of the Vietnam War (provided by the War Department, which paid half their salaries), and plowed forward, head down, believing all the while that the challenges they faced with enrollment were the result of a world gone wrong rather than because of an antiquated approach to what was once a more defensible approach to education. The military model was not broken; it simply needed to be transformed — it needed to evolve into a more nuanced approach to a late 20th century reality.

These failing military schools were boxed into a challenging conundrum, because so many of their loyal alumni had been the beneficiaries of a military education. They had been required as young boys to get up early, clean their rooms, make their beds, line up in "ranks," march into the Mess Hall for breakfast, live by a code of conduct which included a stringent Honor Code, and build the positive habits of highly effective people. They were required to do the tasks that may be unpleasant — like cleaning bathrooms and folding their clothes — which became habits and taught them that part of life is doing what is required of you, pleasant or not. Theirs was a preparation for life after college; and these successful men, leaders in their businesses, their communities, and their families believed that the training at their alma maters — giving them great personal habits, high character, and excellent academic preparation — was the reason for their productive lives. Why would their alma mater ever discontinue that model/philosophy? That would be heresy and possibly the reason to end their financial support for the school they respected and loved.

So military schools had tried to thread the proverbial needle of continuing to provide a World War II backdrop and attempt to ensure the same attention to the detail of military drill, i.e., saber manual, uniform condition and presentation, and immaculate room conditions throughout the day. Parades needed to be of Armed Forces quality. Honor Organizations had to perform with a precision that recalled the halcyon days of the 1950s and 1960s, and the cadets needed to present themselves with the same directness, eye contact, crisp salutes, and focus that their own classmates would have demonstrated in bygone days. The current graduates also needed to be able to gain admission to the most competitive colleges in the country, just as these alumni had. (Note: I remember being told by the President of a well-known military school that he had walked into a Board meeting being more concerned about the quality of the parade the cadets had just performed for the alumni Board members than the fact of the $5,000,000 budget deficit he was about to report to them. He said the Board spent 15 minutes on the deficit and an hour and a half on proper sabre manual.)

On the other side of this difficult equation was the 1970s reality that cadets traveling to and from school in uniform were often chided or insulted for being part of a war machine that was ruinous to the country. These students, who had once taken pride in wearing their uniforms in airports or train stations, were reduced to covering up their uniforms or traveling in civvies, for fear of being shamed publicly. Students in the 1970s were well aware of the social chaos being played out in the colleges and universities. Other prep school students were certainly not getting short haircuts, were not making their beds and cleaning their rooms, or, for that matter, were not marching or even proceeding in an orderly fashion, anywhere.

Even more perplexing, the colleges had begun taking sides on the ROTC experience, and the most competitive universities were removing ROTC programs from their campuses. These were the realities military school administrators faced. Well-appointed and self-disciplined students were not the norm in any schools or colleges. Most private schools around the country were either eliminating their dress codes or reducing the dress code requirements from "coat and tie" to almost whatever was mildly presentable — what some referred to as "neat, clean, and in good repair." New drug and alcohol policies and their consequences were being rapidly added to student handbooks; long hair and facial hair were almost instantaneously deemed acceptable; teachers were no longer addressed as Mr. or Mrs./Miss — and some schools accepted the practice of allowing their students to address the faculty members by their first names or nicknames. All these practices, which later were to become policies, were abhorrent to any and all military schools.

The dilemma was real, but the decision to stay the course and adjust seemed the only viable option. Hair length requirements at military schools became only slightly more lax; the number of times per day the cadets had to march to meals may have been reduced, but not eliminated; and programs like the new cadet system (the process for training new cadets to become fully responsible members of the Corps of Cadets) were shortened, lessening the number of months new students had to wait until they were recognized as full members of the Corps and no longer had to perform all of the duties required of them as "newbies." Watering down (or dumbing down) important military requirements, however, was a challenge for the alumni, and the changes were never really enough for the new students. Why was it important not to walk on campus with your hands in your pants pockets? Why did your overseas cap have to be worn at a 45-degree angle, with the front visor exactly two inches above your eyebrow? Why was it important to have your officers' wrap hanging at knee length or to let your sabre swing freely in the scabbard while you were marching? Because all of this matters if we are going to use the military as our model. The requirements and policies need to be as close to that reality as possible. Otherwise, we would not wear uniforms or carry military accoutrements. Not an easy explanation for a 15-year-old, but a compelling one for an adult…or at least for an alumnus who values and wants to honor the system.

The most compelling experience for me, as I thought about the zero sum game that appeared to have been playing itself out for at least three decades before Pam and I arrived, was a trip Jim Henderson had planned to educate us on the challenges and best practices of military education. They say timing is everything, and that appeared to be the case in our introduction to and arrival at Culver. During the 1980s and 1990s, the nation's military had been involved in a number of actions that had made the military, its leadership, and its philosophy more acceptable, and even more defensible and practicable. Names like Norman Schwarzkopf and Colin Powell were on everyone's televisions and lips, and were a part of the conversation about what leadership looked like lived. Furthermore, the military was on speed-dial for any group dealing with major natural disasters like Hurricane Andrew, because of their self-discipline and organization. The military got things done and it did things efficiently; and that was valuable in situations that needed attention and results. (Note: it was an officer from the Coast Guard who was given the lead on the investigation into the plane crash that claimed John Kennedy Jr.'s life, an appointment that gave the American public a window into what sensible, organized, articulate leadership looked like.)

The military was also getting some credit for having handled thoughtfully the major social problems of racial integration, drug use, and the earliest indications of sexual identity challenges. After all, what organization was a better proxy for the multiculturalism, the diversity, and the requirement for sorting out issues that would impact the quality of its performance than the military? Furthermore, the situation in the Mideast was heating up with radical jihadist attacks led by Osama Bin Laden, and it would not be long before 9/11 and then the controversial WMD (Weapons of Mass Destruction) claims that would lead to the toppling of Saddam Hussein and the start of the Wars of Operation Freedom and on Global Terror. Military was no longer code for militaristic.

This was the backdrop Pam and I had as context, as well as the experiences in our families — Pam's father was a Navy veteran, having served on the aircraft carrier USS Independence, and her uncle had flown for both the RAF and the U.S. in World War II. My family history in the military has been well documented already, but we both had always viewed it with respect and gratitude. We were positively disposed to the military way, but we were relatively uneducated when it came to best practices with leading military institutions. Consequently, our "field trip" to West Point (The United States Military Academy) was especially timely and proved extremely helpful.

Students themselves play a key role in the learning process at Culver.

As it turned out, West Point was not immune from the challenges of competing for the country's most talented students. West Point wanted the best and the brightest to enroll at their Academy, and they had to compete against the likes of Stanford, Harvard, Yale, Princeton, and the great public State Universities, places that did not require military training in addition to academic rigor as part of its educational programming. Consequently, the administration at West Point was reviewing all their policies and practices to determine which of them could be eliminated because they did not contribute positively to the outcomes the Academy sought. There clearly were practices that were extraneous, unpopular and even unsuccessful, some of which served as impediments for some admissions candidates when they made their final decisions about their college destinations. The year before we visited, West Point had undergone its 10-year accreditation as an institution of higher learning and had fared well in the assessment, but there were some notable criticisms. These were important to me since I was looking for a "best practices" experience to fill out the context of my S.W.O.T. analysis of Culver.

I had read the West Point accreditation document with great interest while still studying at Boston University. Unfortunately, at that point in time I had little or no context for this information, but I knew it was important. For instance, one salient point highlighted in the report was that the Committee accrediting the Service Academy reported that the graduates often tended not to be lifelong learners because of the "chug and plug" mentality and schedule of the cadets. Life at the Academy was a series of responsibilities and actions predicated on getting the job done. Every minute was filled with activity, and there was so little time between responsibilities, that the cadets had little time left for reflection. Consequently, they rarely developed the habits of reflecting on the purpose or value of the tasks by which they were consumed.

Furthermore, the report suggested that if everything mattered and had to be addressed with passion and professionalism, how was the cadet to understand what the "value" priorities were? This resonated clearly with me. I had always believed that if I wanted to know what was important to you, I would simply observe how you spent your time. Seeing what you do is a better proxy about what you value than what you say is important to you. So, if in a military system you are asked to spend your time attending to "duties that matter and will advance your development as a leader and a soldier," you need to be certain that those duties do, indeed, result in those outcomes and are meaningful in pursuit of that specific purpose. It all made sense to me, and now we were going to get a look behind the curtain and see how one of the legendary and best-run service academies in the world had responded to these recommendations for their programming.

Our day at West Point was as full of important lessons and interesting experiences as a cadet's day is filled with duties and responsibilities. We met with the Commandant and learned about life in the barracks, TAC officers, and student leadership. We met with the Chief Academic Officer (their Provost) and learned about the importance of an integrated curriculum that included the literature of character and leadership, as well as the important skills of numeracy and science and technology. We met with the BS&L — Behavioral Science and Leadership Department — which housed the leadership curriculum, and there we learned that they were conducting an audit of activities and duties to determine what mattered and should be retained and what should be discarded, because it was irrelevant to building good soldiers and leaders.

All these interviews and presentations were important to our team, but I was most focused on the meetings with the BS&L faculty and trainers. If an institution were to be considered relevant and mission-driven, it had to be certain that what it required you to do resulted in the outcomes it valued and promised to you in the Admissions process. No one wanted to waste time, especially if the wasteful activities appeared to be those whose only relevance was tradition and whose only rationale was "because I said so, or because it has always been this way." What made it worse was that many of the duties or activities seemed tied to the old-fashioned, command-and-control, military approach.

I must admit that my assumption going in was that I would be able to assemble a long list of things to eliminate when our new team at Culver performed a similar audit. I was in for a surprise and for some important education about the Culver system and the cadets' understanding and appreciation of it. I was, of course, expecting some loyalty to the system, especially in matters raised by the new Head of Schools; but I assumed that any "relief" from tedious requirements would be welcomed. I was startled, therefore, when I asked one cadet leader in the Band how relieved he would be if we no longer required new cadets to do square corners in the barracks during the 3–6 months of the New Cadet System. His response was succinct and practical.

"Oh, Sir, that would be a huge mistake. Culver is a demanding place, and for some students new to the Academy, there are many duties and responsibilities that they find challenging and difficult. Square corners, on the other hand, are something even the most timid or uncertain cadet can do. It is important to have something in the military system that everyone can do well."

At this juncture, I had never thought about what did not appear to have any redeeming value as a practice that developed leadership or character, except the marching around the "triangle." I understood that the building of habits was important, but I truly believed that they should be habits that were instructive or constructive in the building of young men. Even if the simple duty of marching was intended to have a cadet reflect thoughtfully on his experience and how and why it was unhelpful to him and to his community, that ideal was often lost on the boy being "punished." What this young leader was telling me was that everyone at Culver starts from a different point, so developing the confidence to do a Culver task and learning to be a part of the Culver system successfully were important, regardless how meaningless the practice was.

This realization was not obvious since these young men, and even the young boys, were a part of a system of completing meaningful tasks, responsibility management, and attention to decorum that made them seem older and more mature than the 14 years of the youngest in the Corps of Cadets. I had to recall my first night visiting the barracks to see the New Cadet System in action on day one. While most of the boys were solidly in control of the requirements of greeting in the halls and doing their square corners in the hallways, a few were clearly out of their comfort zones and were very much young boys away from home feeling the disquieting effects of homesickness and orientation to something new. Upon reflection, the guidance I was receiving informally was meaningful and sensible.

I learned a similar lesson about the value of shining one's uniform regulation black shoes. All new cadets were responsible for having their semi-formal black, laced shoes highly polished at all times. Then, once they entered their second year as Third Classmen (sophomores) they could own and wear "readi-shine" shoes that had a shine built into them. I wondered why we were making the new cadets spend extra time doing something as extraneous as shining their shoes when they were so strapped for time, as it was. Again, an "old man" in the unit explained to me that shining shoes was a vehicle for bonding in the unit. In fact, once new cadets were officially "in" for the night on weekends, they often had "shoe-shining parties" for themselves, during which they discussed their challenges, their experiences, and their best practices for getting the best shine (note: many of the new cadets never traded in their leather shoes for "readi-shines"; they wanted the real thing).

On balance, the trip to West Point was extremely helpful. I observed officers responding to cadets' salutes (a new practice for me) and sat in on planning sessions to organize integrated learning and leadership models in the classrooms. I also received the important reminder that we were not dealing with young men; we were educating boys, and 14-year-olds did not need to be torn down before they could be built up. Our students needed to be given support as well as challenge, and, mainly, they needed to build their confidence around tasks and, then, as leaders. This was why the Culver military system "had to be its own system, not that of West Point or Annapolis."

A few years later, one of our recent graduates returned from his first year as a West Point cadet. He had been a Batten Scholar winner four years earlier, the transformational merit scholarship program conceived of and funded by Frank Batten, Class of '45. For as long as I could recall, this special young man had been dead set on going to either Princeton or Georgetown after Culver. He surprised us all by choosing West Point. During his first return trip to Culver, he made an appointment to stop by my office to check in, and as we spoke about his new school, I felt the need to ask him about whether he felt totally prepared for the U.S. Military Academy experience. He thought for a moment before responding, "I was very well-prepared academically. I was also over-prepared for the leadership training we would receive. There was one thing I was not prepared for: being a soldier. We learned to be leaders at Culver; we were never trained to be warriors. That changes the calculus significantly," he said. "Yes," I remarked, "we do Culver's own brand of military." H.H. Culver would have been proud.

Chapter Nine: Perception is Reality, for Some

We spent the balance of the year seeing the Culver system at work, and our assessment was that the greatest challenge was not the system itself, but rather the perceptions and misperceptions of the system. Any criticism of the system by the students, our families, or the faculty seemed the product of less than professional management of the system and some misunderstanding about it. It did not help that there was a hangover effect among some of the faculty and staff from the Committees that had studied the military system in the late 1980s and had found it wanting, and during the time it had moved away from its JROTC program and the JROTC curriculum.

My early assessment was that Culver may have been struggling with an image problem that had led to a confidence issue. When you feel great about what you are doing, things seem to go more smoothly and what you hope to be true, feels true. When you question your system or the outcomes you are seeking, you see everything with a negative cast, and things are not what you would hope them to be. This was exacerbated by the obvious comparisons with the Prefect System used in CGA. The girls had a leadership system but no marching or drilling — except in the summer. The CGA girls were learning in a system that seemed perfect for them, even though it also took time away from the other responsibilities of serious boarding school students, like studying and participating in extracurricular activities of one's own choosing. The girls had no parades or formal inspection or forming up obligations in the morning; if you were one of the adults who viewed this contradiction as a flaw, there was an obvious remedy: eliminate the military system and replace it with a prefect system.

CGA Council leaders, with elected representatives from all dorms and the senior prefect, meet to discuss agendas, updated results and events at their weekly meetings.

The problem was that many of the older and more influential faculty had never seen the military system in its best iteration. They had arrived at Culver during the Vietnam era and had witnessed the struggles of Culver during this challenging time. And in the era of challenges to all boarding school admissions programs, shrinking resources, and social disruption, any school's profile and product were compromised, forming their opinion of what was, for many of them, the only school experience they had, both unfortunate and unwarranted. This meant that even if the Academy had been operating profitably and well since the challenges facing so many schools in the 1970s, their first experiences were the ones that lingered and shaped their sense of the Academy going forward. What made it worse was that their only experience with the barracks may have been with the "my way or the highway" attitudes of many of the JROTC-era staff. The faculty was lacking in current information and, therefore, they were predisposed to changing what they remembered as a failed system.

CGA senior leaders formally welcoming new girls into CGA who have earned their Crest, which is displayed on their blazers.

The surprising reality was that many of the students saw their school through a very different prism. I recall the first public address we ever heard by the Regimental Commander our first year to a group of alumni who were visiting as part of Alumni Weekend. His message was simple: "Regardless of what you have been told as a leader, you must learn to "sweat the small stuff." He cited the TV commercial popular at the time that counseled you "don't sweat the small stuff," and he said that his experience as a leader had taught him that this was bad advice. As a leader you must sweat the small stuff, because leadership is about taking care of the details and all the minor issues that spell the difference between success and failure. He added that he had also learned that as a leader he did not have the privilege or the right to tell other people what to do. He found out that he worked for the people he led. He was responsible not only for them but also to them; not the other way around.

My reaction was that I wished every faculty member had heard this young man's presentation because he was the product Culver was producing, and in the 30 years before we had arrived at Culver, we had not seen such an outstanding embodiment of leadership in the person or words and actions of a student…or for that matter, from most adults. He had an advantage though: he had received practical leadership training and had earned his position of responsibility, and the students at our former school had not.

The Cadet Code of Conduct was straightforward, but it was not without its challenges for the young men for whom it was created. That was the point: it was aspirational.

The Code of Conduct reads as follows:

> My aim in life is to become the best person I can be. To this end I will strive always to develop my potential to its fullest, physically, intellectually, and spiritually.
>
> To make wise choices, exercise self-discipline, and accept responsibility for my actions.
>
> To place duty before self, to lead by example, and to take care of those I lead.

To treat everyone as I would have them treat me, to fulfill the ideal of service to others.

And to live by the Culver Honor Code: I will not lie, cheat, or steal; and I will discourage others from such actions.

This series of commitments would be considered difficult even for an adult to live by, and surely a world populated by people who led their lives according to these tenets would be a great place in which to live. Asking this of 14 to 18-year-olds is an even greater leap of faith, and some might say a fool's errand. Culver had proved, however, that setting lofty goals for young people and educating them to adopt the habits of personal responsibility and accountability worked. We all understand that young people appreciate having boundaries set for them, and they work best in an environment in which the rewards and punishments for behaviors are clearly articulated and adhered to. Clarity is important in any program in which adolescents are involved, and Culver was a master at providing clarity.

John and Pam Buxton talk with students during a reception in the Alumni Lounge.

Most schools, especially boarding schools, had given up on the behavioral expectations of our parents' generation and on what most adults would consider the reasonable expectations of respect and acceptable behavior during the free-for-all that was the 1970s. To use current terminology, the goal posts had been moved significant-ly during that decade as a result of the social revolution of the late 1960s. The use of drugs and alcohol became prevalent, and schools faced with the inevitable problems related to these substances had two choices — their versions of the "Big Fire," in which you expelled the offenders as part of a "zero-tolerance" policy; or an educational approach which included bringing in organizations to educate the students about the downside of substance use and abuse in an effort to educate them and discourage their use, and providing students with a second chance if they succumbed to the temptation. The latter approach was called the one strike approach, suggesting that students had one additional chance to get it right. Some called this one strike approach the slipperiest of slopes and the beginning of the end of decorum and responsible behavior; but that would only have been true if they concomitantly relaxed the expectations for all aspects of student life. Clearly, Culver had not followed that approach. Culver appreciated the fact that students would make mistakes but also believed that layered on top of the one-strike system had to be the expectations and high-minded goals and objectives of responsible citizenship and leadership.

Commandant Col. Kelly Jordan, US Army Ret., inspects a new cadet leader.

Our early Culver experiences were lining up perfectly with what we had come to value in an educational model. As a teacher, coach, and administrator, I had come to see the benefit and wisdom in setting clear goals, high ideals, and challenging objectives. I had practiced this high challenge/high support philosophy for nearly three decades, so what we were seeing lived in the Culver system made ultimate sense to us. Most important, we realized that whether we were discussing the 1920s, the 1940s, or the 1970s, standards mattered, and students who were prone to getting into trouble had less trouble navigating life if there were boundaries, clarity about "right action," and support for doing the responsible thing. Like the little kids I had played Union soldier with on the Saturday mornings of my youth, young men liked being productively involved, enjoyed being challenged by demanding physical activity, and loved being a part of something bigger than themselves — everyone needed his Union Army.

Rather than simply relying on my personal experience as a youngster or on my personal values as an educator, a coach, and an administrator to decide whether the Culver system was viable, or more importantly, preferable to the systems being pieced together by other schools; I needed research support. I felt strongly that what Culver had been doing for more than a century and was continuing to do when we arrived made sense. In fact, most of the recent literature on leadership, character education, and successful school outcomes was lining up in support of the Culver approach — then and now.

A few examples may be helpful:

In "The Leaders We Deserved (And A Few We Didn't)," Alvin Stephen Falzenberg reviewed the process for evaluating the success of our past Presidents and suggested a new framework. He posited that leaders should be assessed through the lens of "Character, Vision, Competence, Strategy, and Sustainability/Preservation." He explained that a person's character is his or her fate, and that character is a byproduct of honesty, courage, and integrity.

He concluded that in looking at or for leaders, we should seek the following traits:

- A sense of purpose
- How they react to adversity
- How broad is their experience
- Whether they have a sense of integrity
- Whether they seek/reward humility

All of this made sense to me, and furthermore, it aligned perfectly with the Culver Mission, Code of Conduct, and Culver's goals and objectives.

Most students in academic environments were purposeful about their academic performance. Many were similarly committed to their performance in athletics, the Arts, and to their personal extracurricular activities; but these were all self-interested pursuits. There was no "other" in the equation. You might argue that the most special students worked hard for their teachers or toiled in the academic vineyards for the benefit of their parents, who may have been sacrificing so their children could have the best start in life. Most students, however, were worshipping at the shrine of the individual and were busy spending their adolescent years working to build an image of themselves that would be the foundation for the future.

However, there was very little room for service in this model. There was precious little emphasis on purpose or humility. Honesty was glossed over as something everyone had learned in kindergarten, and the word "integrity" was seldom, if ever, mentioned. The notion of coping with adversity had exited the scene with the realities of grade inflation and "no-cut" policies and a ribbon for every entrant philosophies. Adolescence had become a time for the "young flower" to blossom because of good gardening practices, not because of hardihood.

I recall a speech I made during an Open House for the Academies during our first spring. I was becoming more and more encouraged and convinced by what Pam and I were experiencing at Culver. I remember citing a piece I had come across about why one should buy plants from a nursery rather than from a Walmart or grocery store. The logic was that plants in a nursery grow in a natural rather than a protected environment. They endure the cold of winter and the heat of summer. They get dried out and rained on. They develop true resistance to harsh conditions and, therefore, become resilient. The "hot-house" plants, or those that are brought in at night, have not developed the internal strength of those tested in the real world. They may look good, but in stressful conditions, they may not do well. My point was obvious: If your son or daughter comes to Culver, he or she will develop the internal strength and resilience to endure and prevail in any number of circumstances and environments.

Having declared the "What" Culver was offering, it was now time to outline the "Why" and the "How." For that I returned to my research. I could point to the leadership literature and to a book about prosocial development for young men. I could recite the research on leadership training and why practical experience in working with and leading others was the best way to develop the skills of leadership. I realized that the teenage years are a time when the young person is growing and changing at a rapid rate, and that this is the time for intense inward focus. But I also knew it was a time for building the habits of successful leaders, and I believed that one could not accomplish this without clear guidelines and goals and objectives.

Then one day as I was rummaging through my huge and historic desk in that overwhelming Head of Schools' office, I came across a quote from the legendary General Gignilliat, who had written the following in a forward to "Notice, Sirs; Notice, Sirs," the traditional handbook/ training manual/ rule book, and general guide for all cadets. He wrote as follows:

"No boy who wants to do the right thing will go very far wrong at Culver.

Yet for every game there must be a rule book. This, however, is a bit more than a rule book, for it deals not only with obligations but also with opportunities.

Life, after school and college, will require more than is required here. What is required here has been evolved through many years and out of much experience as a preparation for life's varsity game. Some day out of your experience you may rate a seat with the coaches who change the rules of the game. Just now, this is the rule book. Let us play the game according to the rules, both you and I."

Superintendent Leigh Gignilliat at his desk. A major figure in the Preparedness movement of the day, he thrust Culver onto the national stage.

In many ways this preface to the Culver playbook represented the wisdom of the Culver approach. Culver was not interested in providing for parents and students only what they wanted — challenging academics, competitive sports, opportunities in the Arts, and all or most of the comforts of home. In addition, Culver was going to provide for you what you needed by ensuring that you received the training, the habit building, and the guidance you would come to rely on throughout your participation in this real-world Culver system, a system that would help prepare you for life…the varsity game!

Gignilliat understood that young people were struggling to discover and express their independence. They saw the world through a myopic lens and a lens that was self-reflective. When you only gaze into a mirror, you will only ever see what you believe yourself to be. It's hard to be objective about yourself if you are the only evaluator. Gignilliat, and probably his mentor and guide, Col. Fleet, realized that the value of Culver was that when you arrived, it was clear to you immediately that you "had to do Culver." There was no room for creating your own adventure or for writing your own rule book. When you arrived, you symbolically discarded your civilian clothes and put on your Culver uniform. This was not a symbol of your giving up your identity; it was a reminder that your behavior and values now had to be evaluated from a Culver perspective — doing your best to be a person of Wisdom, Courage, Justice, and Moderation — and training to be a leader and of service to others.

In the next few years, I would happen upon or intentionally seek out other warrants that would bolster my commitment to the Culver way. A proverbial light bulb went on when I read "The Global Achievement Gap" by Tony Warner and discovered the work of the Change Leadership Group at Harvard University. Their findings and conclusions supported my developing sense of the efficacy of the Culver model. Both studies concluded that the skills and values needed for success and productivity in the 21st century were evident to those who studied human nature and were conversant with educational philosophy:

- Character (self-discipline, empathy, integrity, resilience, and courage)
- Creativity and an entrepreneurial spirit
- Real world problem-solving
- Public-speaking and communication
- Teaming
- Leadership

This list of outcomes reads like a primer on Culver. This was not the stuff of shrines to individual accomplishment of personal glory that had been described to me when I attempted to explain to a prep school trustee from an eastern boarding school, who asked me to help them understand and then replicate the Culver program on character at their school. When I explained that the Culver system was a fully integrated model built to develop character and that it included intentional scheduling of time for team-work, collaboration and cooperation training, and leadership tasks, he interrupted me and explained that the faculty at his school would never "go for that." He said, sadly, that at his school the students, and even the faculty and Board, believed in and worshiped at the altar of the individual, and that they would never sacrifice individual achievement for character. I realized at that moment that Culver's Trustees had been absolutely right about our society needing exactly what Culver was providing.

The dedication of the Leadership Plaza, located just inside Logansport Gate, in 2002, a gift from the Class of '52 on their golden anniversary. Featured in bronze are the cardinal virtues and Culver values.

The Cardinal Virtues of Wisdom, Courage, Justice, and Moderation were highlighted as the enduring values embraced by a good Culver person. The descriptors of character — self-discipline, resilience, integrity, and empathy — were the specific goals of Culver's two systems — Military (CMA) and Prefect (CGA). Real world problem solving was the essence of a student led leadership program, as was the student run Honor Code. Teaming was the backbone of Culver leadership programs in CMA and CGA; and one learned at Culver that it was the corporate well-being, not individual achievement, that mattered. Furthermore, student-directed programming, in which students not only had a say but also responsibility for outcomes, fostered entrepreneurship, resilience, and creativity. If you ever witnessed a Culver leadership exercise — like a CMA parade or a CGA Leadership Forum — you would understand the importance of good communication skills. These 21st century skills were the perfect vehicle for justifying and building the Culver brand.

CHAPTER TEN: CONSISTENT MESSAGES

Remembering that one of the rules of life is that timing is everything, it follows that saying or doing the right thing at the best possible time will serve you well in all endeavors. You cannot always time things perfectly or as you would wish, as anyone who has tried to time the financial markets knows well, but when it falls your way and the timing is good, you will benefit.

Timing has always been important for Culver. When Culver was first established, the country was looking for educational options that addressed both academic and character development. Culver fit the bill perfectly. Then as the world wars raged, people wanted some insurance that their sons would be able to survive a conflict that threatened to claim their lives. Culver, again, was the answer. During the Vietnam War decade, timing was obviously bad, or at least challenging, for Culver. The great institutions of our country were under fire, and the country was struggling with a recession and consequently a new pressure on private schools — escalating their tuitions. There was a window of hopefulness in the 1980s, but with the stock market beginning to surge and the economy heating up, schools like Culver that continued to believe in the principles that fueled its founding and its growth over a century were not seen as competitive, since the name of the game had changed to college acceptances...period. And remember that the wealthier the population of families attending your school happened to be, the better the chances of their children being admitted to the colleges of their choice, due to development offices wooing these families and admissions offices admitting them in their efforts to boost the endowments that would support the cost of new buildings, the creation of new programs, and the increased need for providing financial aid.

By the time Pam and I were heading to the Midwest, the mood in the country was shifting, and the timing began to look good for any school that could propel its graduates into highly competitive colleges and universities, as well as provide a foundation for strong character, and even better, a preparation for leadership. Also, fortunately, with more students applying to college because of the ease of the application process created by online applications, and due to the heightened interest of international applicants in U.S. colleges, the list of acceptable college destinations was growing exponentially. Excellent state universities and good local colleges were suddenly overrun with qualified and diverse applicants, and what had formerly been considered "safe" schools became extremely competitive and therefore, acceptable as destinations for all students.

Left: Culver Summer Schools students in the riggings of the R.H. Ledbetter ship during sailing instruction courses.

Furthermore, with the increase in terrorist threats and attacks on American targets, and with the military taking on a more positive, peacekeeping role, Culver's leadership programming and its historical connection with the military seemed to be turning sentiment back in its favor. Finally, there were precious few schools even talking about serious and genuine leadership programs in the private school world. On the other hand, there were the same notions about noblesse oblige, and we continued to hear about natural leaders emerging naturally; but the leadership scholars were suddenly focused on teaching leadership and identifying the tenets of true leadership. Military leaders were seen as "can-do" people — women and men who got things done and exhibited excellent character and judgment in their actions and words. We were in a very different place than the one Culver had struggled with only thirty years earlier, so the way was clear for Culver to reclaim its place not only as a school that graduated leaders but also as a leader among schools.

General Gignilliat's reminder about Culver being a two-headed coin of obligation and opportunity rang in our ears as we prepared to complete our first year with a sense of both resolve and confidence. Culver was a school with a differentiated value proposition and a unique delivery system, and we were both excited and amazed by it and only too willing to share this reality with our alumni, faculty, staff, and student body.

Over the course of our second summer and for the next 16 summers, we experienced the joys of the Culver Summer Schools and Camps programming. In 2002, we were party to the celebration of the 100th anniversary of the Naval School, and we saw in real time the evidence of the power of the summer program. It's worth noting that Culver has 19,000 alumni when you count both Summer and Winter School graduates. And if you do the math and consider that the summer programs educate nearly twice the number of participants than in the winter school programs, you can begin to understand the importance of the summer school to Culver. On average, over 1,300 campers and Upper Schoolers arrive on the shores of Lake Maxinkuckee for "fun with a purpose" every summer. We got to meet many of the Naval School graduates we had been hearing about and had the chance to see them in action.

First, there was the planning committee whose job and privilege it was to determine what the celebration of the Summer School Centennial would include. It soon became very clear to Pam and me that we were not simply talking about a weekend in the summer schedule. The celebration would begin with a Florida to Washington, D.C. cruise of the Ledbetter, Culver's three-masted, iconic schooner, and the centerpiece of the Naval School. The cruise would feature a bon voyage, send-off party in West Palm Beach and follow the inland waterway, stopping in key alumni locations along the way to celebrate the history and accomplishments of the Summer School programs. Pam and I attended the send-off and then traveled to be a party to the final destination event in Washington, D.C. In both places Summer and Winter alumni were thrilled that Culver saw the value in sharing the importance of a summer program that rivaled in significance with all the great educational institutions in the country. They were also thrilled to be able to bring their families and friends to learn more about this historic program.

I have spoken at some length about the integrity, humility, and prowess of the members of the Board of Trustees. What I did not understand fully about the Culver

The R.H. Ledbetter, symbol of the Culver Naval School, arrives in Washington, D.C., having completed its journey from Florida to the capitol in celebration of the Summer Schools and Camps' 2002 Centennial.

Board of Trustees was that nearly all the members were also graduates of the Wood-craft Camp — which for most of them was their introduction to Culver. The Chairman of the Board, the President of the Summer Board, and nearly all members of the Executive Committee were former Woodcrafters; most still had their special Woodcraft Dress Coats, filled with medals and badges indicating their accomplishments and rank, hanging in their closets. I surmised once that the secret sauce for success in life was beginning your Culver experience at the Woodcraft Camp as a young boy or girl and then entering CMA or CGA as a young adult.

During the Centennial cruise event, we had the opportunity to meet and talk with the dozens of successful and loyal alumni who treasured their Culver Summer Schools' education and were equally loyal to, proud of, and grateful for Culver. High profile public servants — governors, senators, judges, and mayors, educators, doctors, lawyers, and small business operators — became part of the evidence of Culver's powerful educational reach. I recall vividly listening to Gov. Frank Keating, a Naval School graduate, as he gave the keynote address during the actual Centennial Celebration that summer. I had heard that Evan Bayh, then Indiana's junior senator and a former governor, had graduated from Summer School, but I was not aware that Governor Keating of Oklahoma was also a Naval School alumnus. Governor Keating's message was another "brick in the [Culver] wall." He explained to the nearly 1,500 campers and staffers that his experience at Culver was important to him, because Culver made it clear that they expected him to do something important and to make something of himself. He said, "Culver had expectations of and for me, and that propelled me forward as a leader and as a person of character."

A few summers later the President of Mexico and the First Lady enrolled their two children in the Summer Program. The older of the two was a girl who would be going into the Cardinal Program, and the younger was a boy who would be a Beaver in the boys' side of the Woodcraft Camp. Both were open, positive, and respectful children and good campers; Pam and I delighted in talking with them about their experiences as Woodcrafters.

Our favorite and most meaningful conversation took place with the young boy, who was asked about the most difficult aspect of the program.

"Is it the language? Is it the schedule? Is it the food?"

"No," he responded, to all questions. "It is the leadership. Do you have any idea how difficult it is to get other 10-year-olds to make their beds properly and care about the neatness of the cabin?"

He was delineating between the mundane and the sublime at Culver. He had taken to

Culver's iconic Naval building, with its decks and portholes, serves as the centerpiece for Culver's Summer School centennial, featuring summer leaders in full dress with flags.

heart the slogan — "I can if I will" — that welcomed all Woodcrafters into the Woodcraft Dining Hall. This reminder about right action, perseverance, and leadership was there to inform and then reinforce the notion that you were in control of your future, and that you had the power within you to make important things happen in your life.

On another occasion we were traveling in Spain, visiting our summer alumni and their families. The Culver Summer programs boast students from 40 states and 30 countries, and during most summers there are upwards of 40 students from Spain — so a trip to visit this important country of so many of our campers was appropriate. We were just gearing up to do a major fundraising campaign and had spent the previous six months working with a communications firm to get the best tag line for the Campaign. We were thrilled that just before heading to Spain, we had heard from the firm that they had come up with the best possible slogan. This would be our opportunity to test it.

We were having lunch with a younger graduate who had attended the Naval School as a teenager, and Pam asked him what he believed to be the most important thing he had learned from his Culver experience. Without a second's hesitation he responded: "That's simple…By Example. Everything we learned came in the context of leadership…By Example. Our leaders led By Example, and we were expected to set the example and to lead, always, By Example."

Pam and I broke into smiles: this was exactly what we had spent six months trying to unearth and had just been told by the firm we had hired. They suggested we call the Campaign the "By Example" Campaign, and now this summer graduate (and probably every Culver graduate) could have explained it to us instinctively. This was the essence of the Culver experience; we just were too new to understand that this was a compelling response to the most pressing question: "Why Culver?"

Chapter Eleven: The Leadership Tradition Continues

For seventeen years at Culver, Pam and I had what we considered the best seats in the house to observe leadership by example and in action. These were the warrants we had been seeking. As compelling as the literature on adolescent leadership models was, and as interesting as it was to review the most current educational philosophers and leaders describe as best practices the model we were seeing and living daily at Culver, it was the "proof in the proverbial pudding" that convinced us that every Culver graduate had a right to be proud of his or her school — Summer and Winter. Every time we experienced selfless and remarkable leadership from our students, we would remember the principles of Transformational Leadership documented so clearly by James McGregor Burns:

- Do what works and do what is good.
- Remember that moral dimension must be at the core.
- Be motivated by freedom, commitment, and justice.
- Move from self-centered to altruistic, over-arching values.

Ringing in our ears, as we took in all that Culver had to offer during our 17 years on campus, were the conclusions that noted author and educator, Doug Heath, had made about the qualities of what he called his "Schools of Hope." Heath believed that the gifts all educators around the world wished their children might one day thank them for, were the following:

- Self-confidence
- Joy of learning
- Sense of what is right
- Ability to teach themselves
- Curiosity
- Sensitivity to others
- Compassion

They hoped for students who combined high energy and enthusiasm (what Culver calls "the hope to win, the zeal to dare"), empathy, caring, and respect for others; curiosity and openness to challenges and change; integrity; and commitment and perseverance. They wanted to imbue in their students the traits of adaptability, cooperation, honesty, a self-concept as a member of a global community, and good communication skills. Dr. Heath was describing Culver. But we wanted more objective proof.

Dean Mary Frances "Mai-Fan" England, CAG's (Culver Academy for Girls) original architect and first Dean of Girls, working at her desk and explaining the opportunities and responsibilities to an expectant candidate and her mother during the early days of the girls' program.

Culver Girls Academy had always been the hidden gem in the tiara that was Culver — Culver Military Academy, Culver Girls Academy, and Culver summer schools and Camps. Anytime I mentioned Culver to an acquaintance or to someone I was meeting for the first time, the person would either respond, "What's Culver?" or "Isn't that the school with the black horses and the summer camp?"

No one would ever ask, "Isn't that the remarkable school in Indiana that had the forethought to create a different model of leadership training for their female students when they went coed in the early 1970s?" However, that might have been the most creative and appropriate response that could have been made by any of the greatest schools in the country during the move from single sex schools to coeducational institutions. Culver understood that while its military model was appropriate for young men, it might not serve girls as well. There was precious little research in the late 1960s or early 1970s about Mars and Venus or different genders that would explain the clear differences between the needs of boys and the needs of girls. Carol Gilligan had not yet published her research on gender differences in her landmark book, "In A Different Voice," which did not come out until 1982; and most school administrators and trustees in the early 1970s were focused on application numbers, tuition dollars, and the arguments that would ensue once the historically all-male bastions gave up on their commitment to preserving their current all-male institutions.

Culver was blessed, however, in Mary Frances England, a high-level female educator/administrator who understood that the girls coming to Culver needed something very different from the boys' model. Dean England, or "Mai-Fan," as she was known, was the daughter of longtime Culver Band Director WJ O'Callaghan and so grew up immersed in Culver lore. She had served in World War II as a communications officer with the WAVEs (Women Accepted for Volunteer Emergency Service), and alongside her skills as an English teacher, both at the Academy and the Culver Community Schools, she took on a leading role in the development of young women on campus. With the advent of the summer school for Girls, which launched in 1965, Dean England, the first Dean of Girls in 1971, brought her vision and experience to bear in developing the Culver Academy for Girls, which would change its name four years later in 1975 to Culver Girls Academy.

First, she feared that simply adding girls to what had been an all-boys military academy would label them as second-rate members of the Corps. The boys, she feared, would garner all the leadership positions in such a system, and worse yet, the girls would have to play down a level to be accepted. She wanted an equal playing field, and she wanted her girls to have their own inspiring traditions, narratives, symbols and signs to which to aspire. She made sure that Culver would employ a system of leadership training for the girls that was time honored but not based on the military. As it turned out, she would borrow from both the British and American systems, using the prefect model, in which older students take responsibility for their younger counterparts and are held accountable for ensuring that the younger girls follow, learn, and then assume control of the system.

This prefect system, however, had an American democratic heritage underpinning. The girls' system would use the prefect model to provide an opportunity for caring about and being responsible for others, but the system for governance and organizational leadership would be based on the American form of government — our democracy. The girls would not have rank; they would have positions. They would not be organized by a central nucleus of power and authority residing in the Regimental Commander and his staff and the officers representing the units. They would have a system of committees that would conduct their business independently and then report back to the central committee comprised of the leaders of the various committees. Both models were hierarchical in a sense, but CGA's model highlighted the girls' need for collaboration and cooperation; while the boys' model was more vertical in nature and addressed their need for competition and graduated privilege.

The process that brought us to Culver had been primarily focused on helping us understand and appreciate the more "controversial" of the two systems. Consequently, we walked into Culver without a clear understanding of the quality and magnificence of the Culver Girls Academy. We would not be burdened for long by this ignorance of a truly special part of the Culver experience.

Remember the story of the graduate whose mother called me to recount her daughter's dismay, when on November 11th of her first year at what is regarded as an excellent American college, that there was no scheduled Veterans' Day Ceremony? She was a CGA alumna. A second instance of the same sense of outrage being expressed to a college president because there was no Veterans' Day Ceremony came courtesy of another CGA graduate. Clearly, the messages of integrity and respect, compassion and sensitivity were being received "loud and clear" by the CGA girls, even though their role in the actual Veterans' Day Ceremony was relatively minor compared to that of the boys.

Early in our tenure at Culver, we received an unusual request concerning an Earth Day project spearheaded by a leader of the CGA system. This young woman called to make an appointment with me to discuss her idea of combining Earth Day with an idea she had for a community service project. I took the meeting and was both thrilled and surprised when I heard the scope of her planned undertaking. She was asking for permission to have half a school day off for a large group of girls and boys, so they could refurbish the Culver town park, which over many years had fallen into a state of disrepair.

Her group planned to clean up the site, plant much needed new trees, bushes, and plants, and deliver on a plan for sustaining the effort in perpetuity.

As we talked, I could only use as a reference what I had become used to at our former school. What this young woman was planning was unlike anything I had ever heard proposed by a student. She had imagined, then envisioned, then operationalized a process which would first raise awareness, then recruit others both to the need and to her vision, empower others to complete the tasks necessary to do the work, and following that, to offer the opportunity to others who would help sustain the concept. A last but necessary step would be to gain permission to make it possible and ultimately truly rewarding for those who had planned the entire project.

Was there anything she needed from me?

"Only one thing," she admitted.

"I have already spoken to the Director of Facilities and asked him whether he would be able to loan us some school equipment — saws, shovels, and, yes, a few trucks — if you said it was all right. So, is it possible for us to move ahead with the plan?"

"Absolutely," I said," and Mrs. Buxton and I will be there as volunteers."

Culver students and adults transforming the Culver town beach and park, and more importantly, strengthening community relationships between the Academies and the Town of Culver, during National Youth Service Day in April, 2005.

The following week the genius of this young woman's plan was fully revealed. We arrived at the town park, and the place was already bustling with activity. Volunteers were everywhere, and they were not only Academies' faculty and students but also included town merchants, town leaders, members of the surrounding rural community, a few local school administrators, and her CGA committee members. Even more impressive, however, was the equipment and the materials needing planting. During the preceding months, this young woman had created a campaign to make the case for the improvements in the town park, engage interested citizens in fundraising for the cost of trees and plants, locate bulldozers, tractors, and dump trucks for the work; convince local nurseries to donate or provide products at a fair cost, and provide opportunities for people to create memorials for the town or family members on the park site. This was leadership in action — Culver style.

Only a few years later, another young woman from CGA would make an appointment to see me to ask permission for a project she was planning to do at School. She assured me she would not take too much of my time and began her explanation.

"Mr. Buxton, I need your permission to host a "Relay for Life at Culver."

"What's a "Relay for Life?"

"It's a fundraising event to raise money for the fight against cancer."

"Certainly, I responded. Is there anything you need me to do?"

"No. I think I have it under control."

"Why do you want to do this?"

"My grandfather was recently diagnosed with cancer, and I want to do what I can so other people's grandfathers or other family members do not have to fight the same battle without support."

She left and went to work. She led her CGA teams in an effort the likes of which few people at Culver had ever seen or thought possible. She led the student team that would make contact with townspeople who represented what some called the "four tribes of Culver," because each was so unconnected and often distant, philosophically, from the others. Comprising the tribes were the townspeople, the Academy people, the Lake people, and the farmers. They had different perspectives when it came to town-gown relationships, town politics, personal values, and approaches to life. They sat in different sections of Café Max in the center of town, and for the most part, they kept to themselves.

Our young CGA student's incredibly challenging task was to recruit representatives from these disparate groups to one common vision: the fight against cancer. She surmised that regardless of your socio-economic level, your thoughts about what constitutes progress for the town, your history with the Academy, or your history with town politics; everyone should be able to come together to fight a common enemy. Fortunately, we all had one thing we could agree on…we had to find a cure.

Her resources were the girls and the CGA system. She mobilized 22 individual committees to handle fundraising, team participation fees, entertainment, permission for students to "relay" all night long, minute-by-minute scheduling for the event, participation of the town's high school students, and activities and food for the entire night. There was a Survivors' Dinner which would precede the evening's activities. Speakers for the evening needed to be secured, and participants needed to be encouraged to show up. And, possibly most importantly, the American Cancer Society had to be convinced that it should sanction an event for a high school Relay for Life, which was going to be run by a junior in high school. The conversation between our CGA visionary and the American Cancer Society was notable.

"Hello, this is the American Cancer Society."

"Hello, I am a student at the Culver Academies and we are interested in hosting a Relay event at Culver.

"What's Culver?"

"It's a high school in Indiana."

"We do not recommend that high schools sponsor Relays."

"Oh, we are not really a high school."

"What are you?"

"We are a hybrid; we are more like a college."

"You do understand that you will need to commit to raising a not-insignificant amount of money for the American Cancer Society?

"Yes, of course. We plan to raise $125,000 for the fight against cancer."

"We would suggest a lesser amount — how about $5,000?"

"Our goal is and will remain $125,000."

"$30,000 might be a good compromise?"

"You can put down any amount you choose, of course, but we will raise $125,000."

A moment from the first Relay for Life movement at Culver, which began in 2008 and which would result over time in more than a million dollars raised for the fight against cancer.

Veteran Culver staff member Nancy McKinnis, of the Leadership Department, flanked by Alex Banfich (left) and Romina Clemente, both CGA class of 2008, display a CD of Culver music, "Seasons of the Heart," recorded to raise funds to support the Amani Children's Foundation in Africa.

These may not have been the exact words, but they capture the gist of it accurately. Our CGA student was determined to do what she could to bring a community together around an ennobling cause to make a difference for the Cure. And in the ensuing months, she held meetings to generate the enthusiasm at school, in town, on the lake, and even with potential high net worth donors to make it a reality. She leveraged connections with Indiana's professional football team, the Colts, and brought them on board. She tapped into community talent to arrange for speeches and performances for the event. She arranged with restaurants to provide the food during the evening, and she engaged volunteer ticket-takers, security for the evening, and decorations for the venue. She and her team(s) accomplished all of this, and then waited for the evening of the Relay — hoping for good weather and a great turnout.

Relay for Life began in an emotional and grand style, and the evening began with an even fuller stadium than anticipated. By the end of the evening receipts and contributions totaled $105,000 and they still had pledges coming in for another $25,000. When the window closed for donations at the end of July, this young woman, her classmates and friends had raised $134,000 to fight for the Cure. (Note: In the ensuing twelve years of the event, held annually, more than a million dollars has been raised for the American Cancer Society and has become one of the most reliable and productive Relays in Indiana, including the one held at the University of Notre Dame.)

The third jewel in this list of warrants is the creation of the Leadership Committee for Africa, another creation of the girls of CGA. One afternoon the girls heard Oprah Winfrey discussing her work to support AIDS orphans in Africa. They became interested, and after discussion among themselves and with their advisor, they presented the idea to Pam and me. Their concept was to create a series of initiatives to raise funds to support orphaned babies in Kenya. Their hope was to make a difference in the lives of these orphans, to provide leadership training for an African leadership school called Christel House, and to engage in a local agricultural project, creating a sustainable food source for communities in Africa where hunger and starvation were rampant. Christel House was the creation of Indianapolis philanthropist, Christel DeHaan. Our students would be working with local farmers in Indiana to grow the crop, amaranth.

They dug in with the zest and zeal typical of all Culver students and did their research. Then they began to create the network that would support these three initiatives. I remember when they told me the Academy would be welcoming the founder and executive director of the orphanage in Nairobi and the Amani Foundation to our campus. I have no idea how our students made this connection, but the people responsible for saving so many lives were here to accept the funds generated by LCA's fund-raising efforts, primarily from the sale of jewelry made from Kenyan beads, which the students had made themselves and sold during the summer at local Farmers' markets. The check was for $10,000.

The Leadership Committee for Africa began in 2004 as an initiative to support orphaned children and morphed into a multi-faceted program to teach support for needy children by developing leaders in and for African communities.

The following year their fund-raising was equally productive, but this time they made their donation personally during their trip to Africa to devote time to training the students of the Christel House School in Africa. They shared the practices and tenets of good leadership with these young leaders, who aspired to be leaders in their own country. Finally, their work with Amaranth bore fruit — no pun intended — once they connected with a laboratory in Florida that was experimenting with sustainable food sources and began experimenting with variations of the Amaranth plant. Who knows where this will end up? We never underestimated our Culver students!

When we recite the gifts, we hope to give our children: a sense of what is right, sensitivity to others, cooperation and respect for others, creativity, commitment and perseverance, and seeing oneself as a member of a global community. It's Culver Girls Academy, Culver Military Academy, and Culver summer schools & Camps.

CHAPTER TWELVE: COMMITMENT, DETERMINATION, AND RESILIENCE

During our second year at Culver, Pam and I accompanied the Hendersons to the Presidential Inaugural Parade in Washington, D.C. The Black Horse Troop at Culver first participated in the Inaugural Parade as guests and escorts of Vice President Marshall of Indiana, during the Presidential Inaugural Celebration and Parade for President Woodrow Wilson in 1913. They did so again in 1917, and returned for President Eisenhower's second Inaugural in 1957. After that event and then, every year there was an Inaugural Parade — with the exception of President Clinton's first term Inauguration in January 1993 — Culver Troopers were invited as participants in the parades. The Culver Girls Academy Equestriennes, CGA's most accomplished riders, were invited to President Reagan's second Inaugural Parade in 1985. The Equestriennes and Black Horse Troop now represent the school equally when participating in the Parades.

Culver's first presidential inaugural participation took place in 1913, escorting vice president Thomas Marshall of Indiana.

Back to January 2001, we traveled to the capitol, attended a Culver Club event the evening before the parade, and woke up at the crack of dawn, a good Culver practice, to watch our students ride down Pennsylvania Avenue. The morning was cold and wet, and we left the hotel early to get a good seat from which to witness what would be a first for Pam and me. We had visited the stables on numerous occasions to watch the riders practice under all kinds of conditions. We had even gone on a practice ride with them through the Town of Culver, a training ride to get the horses and their riders used to noise and traffic — though all knew there was a huge difference between Culver and D.C. We had watched as younger Troopers had banged on trash cans and waved black plastic bags in front of the horses to prepare them for any surprises they might encounter on the actual day of the Parade. Culver was trucking 80 horses to Washington and entrusting to a large group of high school students the responsibility of navigating one of the most raucous parade routes in the country. That was a lot of trust; but if General Gignilliat could send off a group of young men to rescue a town full of stranded citizens from a raging flood, we should probably feel comfortable with the risks posed by a parade.

Left: Culver's invitation to the World Equestrian Games of 2010, the first time that event was held outside Europe, denotes the school's stature in the equestrian world. Here, members of Culver's Equestriennes take part in the event's opening.

What had struck Pam and me as remarkable was the reality that to be fully prepared for the Inaugural Parade, the Troop and Equestriennes had to begin their own and their horses' training in late August, a full five months before the Parade was scheduled and four months before any of the eventual participants would even receive their formal invitation. This meant that the students could have practiced for 120 days without any guarantee of being invited. This Parade is planned by the winning party, which means that invitations are given on the basis of political priorities. If the Party responsible for issuing the invitations is pressed for space in the Parade because of the sizes of the groups of those on the "absolutely must be there" list, a group like Culver can be eliminated at the last minute. But the students understand the reality of this process of choice and they accept it. This is the openness to challenges and change we want to see in all young people, another value of the Culver system.

The Equestriennes and Black Horse Troop pass the presidential viewing stand during the 2013 inaugural parade.

Now we were sitting on the Parade route looking for some protection from the wind, rain, and cold temperatures. We found a coffee shop and managed to make our hot beverages last for an hour, but we were then back in the elements and feeling the effects. The hours passed and finally, as daylight was fading, we received word that the Culver Black Horse Troop and CGA Equestriennes were on their way and should be passing us while there was still light. That news motivated us to tough it out in anticipation of what we knew would be a proud moment for the students and for us.

Before we knew it, the American flags every rider carried, and the enthusiastic cheers of the crowd signaled the arrival of this incredibly special group of young people. Our students had arrived at the stabling site at 5 a.m. that morning, and now, eleven hours later, they were acknowledging the newly elected President of the United States with more dignity and pride than is imaginable, given the fact that they were literally stuck to their mounts. Their tears were frozen on their cheeks, but their smiles were genuine. They had persevered, and they embodied the confidence, self-discipline, enthusiasm, high energy, and the self-concept as a member of the global community as they represented their countries, themselves, and Culver so well. Our tears were frozen in place as well. We need more Culvers in this world if we want young people to be "fit for their future."

This experience made me recall how different the conclusions of my doctoral research would have been if I had only been able to experience Culver and its spectacular programs before committing myself to the analysis, almost sight unseen. My research question had been: "What is preventing a school that has done all the things suggested by best practices in education, applied the most current adolescent research to its programming, and utilized the information coming out of the most cutting-edge gender research, from realizing its full potential?"

What I was beginning to understand was that while Culver needed attention to some of its policies and practices and clearly needed to work on the language it used to describe its mission, it had every aspect of quality 21st century education soundly in place. What it lacked was exposure, the confidence to declare its rightful place as a leader in education and one of the great schools in the country. I was more certain of this the more our Culver experiences demonstrated that the educational experts were correct in explaining what young people needed from their education and from the schools. Culver was providing it.

A few years into our tenure at Culver, Pat Bassett, the former Executive Director of both ISACS (the Independent Schools Association of the Central States) and NAIS (the National Association of Independent Schools) published a piece on 21st Century competencies. He listed six of them and referred to them as the Six C's:

- Creativity

- Character

- Critical thinking

- Communication

- Collaboration

- Cultural competency or Cosmopolitanism

Most educators would agree that the majority of excellent schools do a pretty good job teaching young people to be creative, at least academically and intellectually. They all claim to be leaders in the critical thinking movement, and many do, more so on the academic front. Some are better than others on this skill, but many are doing an excellent job training their students to be good written and verbal communicators; and by dint of the world becoming smaller, flatter, and more crowded and navigable, cross-cultural competency is a reality that is difficult to avoid. But the development of character and a commitment to teaching and encouraging collaboration are harder claims to make.

The report card on most schools is that while they are doing well on the academic front with most of these competencies, they cannot make claims on two of the most important — character and collaboration. Remember the conversation I had with the Board member from an elite private boarding school who called, asking for what I would label the "Just Add Water" approach to building character — an approach that would entail simply making room in the academic curriculum for such programming.

His response was that the faculty would never support anything that interfered with the academic quest their students were on.

I had explained to this prep school board member that the program to create leaders of character required a commitment to collaboration and teaming. His response, one that has echoed in my ears for years, was that, at his school, everyone worshipped at the shrine of the individual and individual achievement, so a character and teamwork commitment could not possibly be in their future planning. He wanted the shortcut version of the solution to their need.

You see, most people believe that a school can elicit the good character traits in people by reminding them not to cheat, steal, or lie. If you do your own work and keep away from others' property, you are doing what is right. Some schools go farther and suggest strongly that its students should act proactively if they see something bad happening — like bullying or discrimination. Often, however, these expectations are set up to protect the identity of the one reporting the transgressions, which means it really doesn't take too much courage to be a person of character in these instances and removes the character part from the equation. And if you accomplish something as a team, how are you going to get the adulation and credit you rightly deserve for your significant role in the outcome of the project or the game?

It is hard to make room in the curriculum of a school for all this training, but it became clear to me that if you do not have a practical training ground for practicing these competencies, you are dealing solely with abstractions…ideas and concepts but not reality. Someone must have said that the difference between theory and reality is that only one of them is real! Back to Aristotle: If we are what we repeatedly do, then it is the repetition that makes our intentions habitual and engraves them into our character. Maybe the Six Cs should be changed to the Single C — Culver.

Harvard Business Review published a number of monographs on leadership, and at the time of our moving to Culver, the topic of leadership began to receive significantly more attention (another "good timing" coincidence). The Review reprinted a number of its best Leadership papers, and while I could quote a number of them to make my point, I selected one by Daniel Goleman entitled "What Makes a Leader?" Goleman's thesis was that selecting leaders was not a matter of finding the person with what many consider the "right stuff": charisma, brains, experience. Goleman determined that "Effective leaders are alike in one crucial way: they all have a high degree of emotional intelligence." In his research, he determined that "emotional intelligence proved to be twice as important as the others [technical skills and I.Q.] for jobs at all levels, but in an increasingly important way at the higher and highest levels of a company.

Goleman went on to identify the Five Components of Emotional Intelligence:

- Self-Awareness
- Self-Regulation
- Motivation
- Empathy
- Social Skill

While many of the definitions and traits of these components of Emotional Intelligence will resonate with Culver men and women as byproducts and outcomes of their participation in the Culver system, what is more intriguing is Goleman's answer to the question, "Can Emotional Intelligence be learned?" He is balanced in his response but clear that while the level of one's emotional intelligence is a result of both nature and nurture, "research and practice clearly demonstrate that emotional intelligence can be learned." He goes on to explain that emotional intelligence is born largely in the brain's limbic system, which governs feelings, impulses, and drives. Research indicates that the limbic system learns best through motivation, extended practice, and feedback, all elements of the Culver leadership programs. Once again, I was drawn back to my meetings with the alumni we had met on our travels and the Board members we had come to know so well. This was another product of the Culver experience, and possibly the reason so many Culver graduates — summer and winter — were successful leaders in their businesses, their communities, and, especially, for their school.

It was becoming clearer by the day that great 21st Century schools, like Heath's "Schools of Hope," were committed to developing people of character who would be caring, respectful, productive members of a team, know how to solve problems, could and did think critically, worked hard, and told the truth. Socrates said, "The way to gain a good reputation is to endeavor to be what you desire to appear." That must have been in Colonel Fleet's mind as he imagined this system for Culver and articulated to his faculty and staff why repetition was important in developing the habits one needed to be a responsible citizen for the Republic. Pam and I were seeing daily, just as we had experienced on that first day of Summer Camp, that all Culver people — adults and students — were about the business of training to become the people they wanted to be and the people of character that society needed. This was the grand experiment, and it was working. More people needed to know about this place.

Chapter Thirteen: Leadership Requires Action and Results

Once Pam and I had settled in — just barely — I began to hear almost immediately from representatives of two of Culver's signature programs: The summer schools and Camps and the Black Horse Troop. The summer schools and Camps have already been given significant attention in this primer on Culver, but I should mention that the first formal meeting I had in early July, that first week in the office, was with the President of the summer schools Alumni Association. He explained to me that the summer program, which I would come to see as one of the "crown jewels" of Culver, was not getting appropriate attention from the winter school and its Board and Administration.

He cited as his example the fact that when he called the early summer meeting, no one from the administration showed up. I explained what I imagined were the challenges of any early summer meeting, with the tight turnaround from the end of the winter school year and the beginning of the summer schedule, but I assured him I would investigate his concern. I was, of course, absolutely clear with him about the positive impressions both Pam and I had formed from our experience with the summer programming since our arrival. What I would come to learn in the years that followed was that while this was a fair criticism, it was, more importantly, another example of living in a vacuum.

I never believed that the summer schools and Camps experience was inferior to the winter school's. It certainly was different, but there had to be a difference. The summer schools and Camps was focused primarily on leadership through the acquisition of skills; and while summer coursework had been a hallmark of the summer school — Culver offered courses in all the major academic subjects and later added instruction in world languages and courses focused on synthesis and analysis — the focus was on teaching "Woodcraft" and "Naval" or "Horsemanship" and "Aviation" skills as a pathway to learning leadership. The winter school, on the other hand, required all its students — CMA and CGA — to handle full academic loads, in addition to assuming leadership responsibilities, participating in extracurricular activities, and engaging in community programming.

Furthermore, the summer school was an eight-week program originally, and later in its history it went to a seven-week program and has been a six-week program for the last 40 years. The winter school had a nine-month calendar. The summer school had been created as a vehicle for providing young people a summer experience that was both exciting and fun, as well as purposeful. The winter school was equally focused on leadership, but its heavy academic requirements were both challenging and time consuming. There were clear differences. Most of the summer and winter participants attended only one program and not both. Therefore, there was little opportunity for them to develop a perspective on the other program.

All that summer school students knew about the winter school was that their summer campus and all the buildings they used were exactly the same as those used by the students of CMA and CGA. Beyond that, they did not have much information about the winter program nor were they particularly interested in it. The summer schools and Camps were not like a little brother or sister who wanted to be included in the older siblings' activities; they were more like cousins who didn't get together that often but liked, or at least appreciated and respected, one another.

Things were slightly different for the summer schools Alumni Association Board of Directors, whose primary goal was to serve as an instrument of communication between the alumni they represented and Culver's leadership. Since they were privy to the winter school's finances and operational reports, the Summer directors saw the discrepancies between the two programs financially and wondered why the summer school receipts should be used for the well-being of the winter school program rather than to provide more support for the Summer programs. Clearly, from my point of view, this was a problem of not seeing the whole picture. What I saw was that the summer school supporters needed to be given the bigger picture and provided language to explain what was happening. It was always disappointing to hear a summer school alumnus or alumna say, "I went to Culver, but I just went to the summer school." There was no "just" about their experience or the commitment and knowledge they took away from the program, and the rest of the story (Paul Harvey once again) was that the success of both the summer school and Woodcraft Centennials in 2002 and 2012 respectively, made it clear to all alumni that there was no reason to wonder about the quality and importance of their summer schools and Camps. The operative expression became "One Culver."

The situation with the Troopers was somewhat different. When I had my first meeting with a well-placed and clearly disgruntled Black Horse Troop alumnus, I wondered if he was simply using a 1940s lens to evaluate a year 2000 reality. For background, the person sitting across from me in the Superintendent's Office in the Legion Building was a highly respected and clearly successful individual. He was one of the leaders in one of the legendary classes of Culver, and he was as loyal and committed to supporting Culver as anyone Pam and I had met. He loved Culver and he loved the Troop; and his purpose in meeting with me was to explain to me how and why the Black Horse Troop was synonymous with Culver, and that its well-being and success were integrally tied to Culver's success.

I recall being impressed by the reasonableness of the person providing this explanation and how measured he was, even though he obviously had real passion for the "Cavalry" program. I also remember thinking that if what he said was true, we have work to do; and if we cannot make the improvements and commitments he is suggesting, the Black Horse Troop alumni might just secede from the Alumni body; i.e., take their footballs (boots and saddles) and go home. He was not threatening; he was sincerely concerned that some of Culver's most loyal supporters were Troopers, and he knew they would support improvements to Culver's premiere "leadership laboratory."

Coming into this meeting as a newcomer, I was totally unprepared for the avalanche of information about the shortcomings of the current Troop and Horsemanship programs. I had ridden horses on and off for most of my life. It seemed neighbors always had a pony or a horse that needed exercising, so although I was never formally trained in the horsemanship arts, I could ride and enjoyed riding whenever the opportunity arose. Pam and I spent our vacations on horseback in the Rockies, and we both appreciated horses and the people who cared for them. Imagine our excitement when we learned that Culver stabled many dozens of horses and offered training in cavalry skills for CMA and in showing and jumping for CGA. The black horses looked impressive, and the parades and horse shows were amazing for a "high school," even a "hybrid." To be told the horsemanship program was in a state of disrepair, my response was, "Compared to what?"

One definition of leadership is a 120-pound adolescent partnering with a 1,200-pound horse for a positive result, demonstrated here by Culver's Equestriennes.

What happened next went a long way toward demonstrating to me that the Troopers really had learned their leadership lessons especially well. They volunteered to form a special committee to evaluate the current state of the Horsemanship program, to make recommendations for improvements, and then to lead the effort to ensure those improvements were planned and funded. This was not a group of men and women who wanted to make recommendations and leave the solving to the Academy. They were the Academy, and they certainly planned on being part of the solution, in every possible way.

Much of this was especially impressive to me because it was another instance of "By Example" leadership. I must say, however, that I was not surprised about horses being the perfect vehicle for teaching leadership. When a young person weighing 120 pounds is working with an animal weighing 1200 pounds, there better be a partnership between the two, or the larger entity will carry the day. If that young person has not learned the importance of respecting his or her partner, treating the partner well and caring for its needs, and making sure the partner is not being asked or directed to do something dangerous or ill-advised, he or she has not learned some of the most important tenets of leadership. All Culver Troopers and Equestriennes learn these skills and principles in their work with the horses. I had learned these precepts as a young rider, but I had learned them intuitively. Culver was teaching these leadership skills explicitly.

As the school entered into this partnership with its horsemanship alumni, I realized I needed to do my homework as well. I knew that General Gignilliat had been responsible for purchasing the Academy's first black horses and cavalry gear when a Cavalry Troop in Cleveland was disbanding. He seized on what he identified as a great opportunity to accomplish two things: to fill out his military model with its own cavalry unit and, just as important, to provide another method for teaching leadership. Gignilliat was a horseman, and he understood how important the lessons learned on the back of a horse could be for a leader-in-training. I decided to do my own research to understand more fully the story of the Troop.

The 1911 Catalogue for the Academy has a separate section entitled "Cavalry." The explanation begins with a quote from the noted educator and educational theorist, Horace Mann:

> "All through the life of a feeble-bodied man his path
> is lined with memory's gravestones, which marks
> the spot where noble enterprises perished for lack of
> physical vigor to embody them in deeds."

It continues with the solution: The Cavalry Department at Culver Military Academy, will "supply every possible means for the perfect development of the boy." The literature goes on to point out that "everyone knows, including the best physicians, that horseback riding is the most healthful of all physical exercises, since it brings into use every muscle of the body and every faculty of the mind."

To become a skilled rider, one must develop/possess the following traits:

- Physical strength
- Agility
- Patience
- Perseverance
- Resilience

Riding horses at Culver demanded "the use of every muscle of the body and every faculty of the mind."

If you are a slow-moving timid boy, Culver will help you acquire greater energy and better courage.

If reckless or immethodical, the Cavalry will teach you to become more careful and systematic.

The Cavalry section concludes:

> "The boy who masters the art of riding as taught in this Academy will have acquired a thorough knowledge of and a taste for beneficial exercise that will follow him through life." There was no fine print, but if there had been, it would have added that only the most proficient of the students would be enrolled as members of the Black Horse Troop. Then, not long after this was published, the requirements were changed to include the language "…and of the best character."

Cavalry Drill at Culver Military Academy, Culver, Ind.

All this information was bringing into focus the power and influence of the Troop. During our first few years at Culver, a disproportionate number of Regimental Commanders — the one cadet each semester selected to be the highest-ranking cadet and the cadet who would take on the greatest responsibility for the Corps of Cadets and literally run the military program — were Troopers. Every year the school conducted its Annual Review for the Corps of Cadets, which at one point had been a part of the Inspection the government conducted of its ROTC schools to ensure that quality standards of military protocol were being observed. In most of our first years, the Troop won this competition so many times consecutively that instead of calling the process the Culver Annual Review, they referred to it as the "Cavalry's Annual Reward."

We formed two groups of alumni to advise us and when we factored in the thoughts and professional responses of both the Committee of the Horse and the Horsemanship Advisory Council, it was abundantly clear that you do not get to do the Cavalry at Culver in anything but a first-rate fashion. The giants of the Troop, leaders like General Gignilliat, Colonel Rossow, Colonel Whitney, and Major Townsley, and so many others who led and supported that program, would not have had it any other way. Yet, they never said, "If we cannot do better, we will all fold our Cavalry tents." Nor did they say that "If you cannot do better, you better figure it out." They said, "Let's work together to figure this out." Period. No alternative. This was another example of the resolve that leaders show. All their mental faculties, patience, perseverance, and grit were coming to the fore. These Horsemanship representatives, and all the Regimental Commanders and Troop commanders with whom we had worked in our first few years, had convinced us that the leaders of the Troop were forceful, loyal, respectful and determined.

All this said, the true measure of the power and quality of a person's or a group's leadership is in the results and solutions it produces. In the case of the two committees I have referenced, the results were typically impressive:

2009 saw an unprecedented renovation of Culver's Robert C. Vaughn Equestrian Center and Jud Little Riding Hall, making the school's equestrian facilities some of the finest in the world.

- A revitalized horsemanship program in both the Summer and winter schools.

- A renovated Riding Hall.

Both the Equestriennes and the Black Horse Troop represented Culver at the prestigious World Equestrian Games in 2010.

- New stables for nearly 100 horses.

- A sustaining endowment for Horsemanship, to include funds for the purchase of appropriate horses, i.e. black horses.

- Scholarships for Troopers and Equestriennes.

- An invitation and a trip to the World Equestrian Games.

- Three more invitations and trips to Presidential Inaugural Parades.

- A relationship with the Household Cavalry Mounted Regiment in the UK to provide an instructor for an annual instruction visit.

- Inclusion of a western riding program.

Looking back on our time at Culver, it is understandable that so many people, when asked if they know what Culver is, respond, "Oh, is that the place with the Black Horses?" It also makes it unsurprising that the young people who rode in those freezing conditions in the Inaugural Parade our first year showed the self-discipline, the pride, the perseverance, the character, and the grit characteristic of Troopers, Equestriennes and Culver people in general.

Chapter Fourteen: The Art of Culver

When the S.T.E.M. (Science, Technology, Engineering, and Mathematics) movement was well-established, educators looked more closely at the research on the traits needed to navigate the 21st century and added an "A" to the equation for educational priorities, which changed the acronym to S.T.E.A.M. the "A," as we now know, stood for Arts. Generations of public school students surely remember bringing home a flute or trumpet, and sometimes even a tuba, so they could practice for the school's music program. Those days may have been decades ago, but I was reminded of them when the STEAM discussion surfaced once again, as our grandson asked Pam and me to listen to the flute solo he was preparing for a school concert.

Culver's rich horsemanship and fine arts traditions meet in the innovative equine sculpture program.

Remember the Six Cs or competencies required for this new century, and consider whether you improved your creativity, critical thinking, communication skills, collaboration, character, and possibly even cosmopolitanism while spending hours trying to make that instrument sound like what it was and finally make music with it. Learning to be a musician or just a "junior screecher" in the elementary school concert is challenging, and the repetition of learning the scales, the habits formed during hours of practice, and the self-discipline required to master the craft all apply to the development of a successful and accountable 21st century citizen. The Arts, however, do not refer only to music. Drama, dance, drawing and painting, and sculpture are also included in the artistic activities, and all of these build the same competencies. Leaders need to be good critical thinkers. They need to be able to communicate their message to an audience. They need to be creative. The need to pay attention to detail, i.e., "to sweat the small stuff." They need to be able to learn from failure, and they need to work hard and follow their passion. Finally, they need to be persistent, determined, and resilient.

Legendary actor the late Hal Holbrook CMA '42 exemplifies the longstanding prevalence of the arts at Culver, and often spoke of his Culver experience inspiring his work in theater.

When Pam and I arrived at Culver, we certainly expected to see people marching, and saluting, and even riding horses, but we had few expectations about the emphasis the Academy would be putting on the Arts. My research had documented that both summer and winter programs had a Band to play for its parades, but we expected far more emphasis and pride being placed on military activities than on artistic performance. We should have begun to understand the central role of the Arts at Culver when our contact person and guide for our first visit was the Head of the Fine Arts Department. Imagine our surprise when the centerpiece for the opening of the summer schools and Camps program was the Naval Band!

Then we were informed that every Saturday evening the Woodcraft Campers who were participating in the Indian Lore program would be performing a play depicting the values and lessons learned from the Native Americans who had inhabited the area, and the country as a whole, before Culver was founded. The play would feature authentic Native dances and Woodcrafters playing the roles of young boys and girls on the journey to adulthood. The performance took place at the Camp's Council Fire, a theatre in the round that accommodated all members of the Woodcraft Camp who filed in for the weekly event (more than 800 people were regularly in attendance on a Saturday night). These were thinly disguised "morality plays" intended to celebrate Native American culture and teach the Woodcrafters the lessons of character, self-sufficiency, and respect.

Pam and I rarely missed a Council Fire if we were on campus. The Woodcrafters also had their own marching band — the Woodcraft Drum and Bugle Corps — and this group performed twice a week, once during the weekly Retreat and then again

The Woodcraft Camp's renowned Drum and Bugle Corps perform at a summer parade.

in front of an audience of parents, counselors and friends of about 1500 people on Sundays. This group even had the honor of playing and marching with the legendary Naval Band during the Sunday parade. And every summer the debate at most of the restaurants, cafes, and stores in the Town of Culver was the "quality and numbers of the Naval Band this summer." That was the bellwether for the viability and future of the Summer Program. It truly mattered, and the reason was that the Band is literally and figuratively the heartbeat of any military program. Music mattered, and the arts mattered at Culver.

After we had been at Culver for a few years, we began to meet some of the alumni who had lent their significant art collections to Culver for the celebration of the Academy's Centennial in 1994. The two major art donors were both graduates of the late 1930s and the early 1940s. One was the owner of a professional football team and the other managed a highly successful paper company and has a street in his city in Alabama named for him. One possessed arguably the best American western art collection in the country, while the other

may have owned the most celebrated American art collection under one roof. Both were staunch supporters and lifelong devotees of Culver. Jim Henderson and others explained to us that as the Centennial approached, committees of alumni debated the best way to showcase the Academy and celebrate Culver's success. There were to be a number of events, but the focus would be the sharing of the artwork of nearly every one of America's greatest painters, works that resided, remarkably and notably, in the collections of a handful of Culver graduates.

The Crisp Visual Arts Center, which opened in 2011, represents Culver's acute commitment to the arts and includes beautiful gallery, studio, auditorium, and storage space befitting the school's remarkable visual arts collection.

One of the more interesting narratives surrounding the celebration was the reaction of the two well-known and highly regarded museums that had been asked if they would house the collections during the Centennial. Each responded politely to the question of whether the museum would be able to show the works for the proposed period of time, but it was clear from their reactions that they were not in the business of accepting a mere high school's collection for a major show. Maybe those asking should have added, "That Culver is not really a high school; it's a hybrid!" Their response changed quickly once Culver sent them a listing of the paintings that would be on loan for the exhibit, so they could make an informed decision. The affirmative response by the two museums was immediate and accompanied by their request to retain the paintings for a longer period of time so their patrons could see this remarkable collection.

The Culver Centennial exhibit was entitled, "American Traditions" and so many quality paintings and sculptures were accepted (150) that the exhibit had to be displayed at three Indianapolis area museums simultaneously. Over thirty-five alumni agreed to lend works that met the very high-quality standard of the museums.

Bret Waller, then the head of the Indianapolis Museum of Art, wrote in the catalog, "This is one of the finest exhibitions of its kind ever seen here. How and when the art collecting bug found its way into Culver's drinking water supply, Lake Maxinkuckee,

Part of the 1994 celebration of Culver's centennial was an acclaimed exhibition of art from Culver alumni collections, held at three prominent Indianapolis art museums. A comprehensive and collective catalog (right) of works from the exhibitions was published by the Indianapolis Museum of Art in conjunction with Culver.

remains a mystery beyond our ability to solve. The evidence of the exhibition documented in these pages proves beyond all doubt Culver can count among its alumni some of the most discriminating and devoted art collectors in this hemisphere…one thing that characterizes the collections of all of these Culver alumni is their commitment to quality."

Years into our career at Culver, the leader of the Culver Legion proposed a "One Culver" event for all Summer and Winter families and alumni in the Chicago area and from the Upper Midwest at the Art Institute of Chicago. His rationale was that Culver people would appreciate having the opportunity to see the special exhibit that was being shown at the time and that it would be great to bring Summer and Winter graduates together as a single entity. The event turned out to be the best attended off-campus Culver event ever hosted. Maybe art was somewhere near the center of the Culver experience.

It's worth noting that two of the four building projects funded during the By Example campaign were done in support of the Arts.

We received similar feedback on the importance of our "horse arts" (as we had come to call them) from alumni/ae everywhere. Horseback riding was an art and such a great vehicle for teaching leadership that there is agreement, as Teddy Roosevelt quipped, "It's hard to believe how much good the outside of a horse can do for the inside of a boy or girl."

Consider the perseverance, the self-discipline, the respect, and the creativity one

Culver's Dancevision program dates to 1977 and has, from its inception, particularly showcased the talents of female students.

learns in jumping, eventing, polo, and, especially, in Inaugural Parades or even in Sunday Parades throughout the year at Culver. The difference between the arts and the horse arts, however, was that in horsemanship it was often both the instructor/director and the horse that made all the difference. We heard stories of the special relationship between a student and his or her horse that made being away from home in a demanding environment bearable at first and ultimately fun and extremely beneficial.

What became increasingly clear to us was that all the programs at Culver worked in an integrated fashion in the commitment to teaching leadership and service. Culver programs included excellent academics and wonderfully creative and competitive opportunities in extracurricular activities. It was Culver's mission of teaching leadership and responsible citizenship by developing the whole person — mind, body, and spirit — that made Culver fully differentiated and important to the world of education and to society at large.

Theater continues to be a vibrant part of Culver's fine arts offerings. Among the renovations to the Eppley Auditorium which accompanied the creation of the Steinbrenner Performing Arts Center, one of the major arts-related building projects of the 2000s, was the addition of a state-of-the-art performance space.

Chapter Fifteen: Leading By Example

Pam and I were thoroughly convinced, possibly after only a few months, but certainly after a year or two into our new lives in Culver, that Culver was a place with which alumni/ae and their families had a sincerely committed relationship. Remember the words of the Board Chairman who said to the students and faculty and staff at that Opening Convocation, "Culver will capture your heart for life in the process." The Trustees were willing to drop whatever they were doing to get to a meeting in Culver, to take a call, to set up a meeting, or to host an event. Alumni/ae talked effusively about how much their Culver experiences had influenced their lives, their careers, and even their families.

One of our favorite stories involves three graduates, one of whom is an employee. The Class of 1953 was coming back for its 50th Reunion, and I was scheduled to meet with the Class leaders to discuss some of the key prospects in the Class — people who could help them break the one million dollar mark set by their "older brothers" and mentors in the Class of '52. The Class of '52 had broken the one million dollar mark the previous year by raising $1,000,052.52 and 1953's leadership was committed to coming in at $1,000,053.53. To reach this goal, they needed to be both strategic and tactical in their research on the Class. Their pressing yet sensitive question for me was whether I thought it would be all right to meet with one of their classmates who had been one of the top five givers in the class annually. The issue was that he was currently working as an hourly employee in Culver's Food Service Department, and if what they were asking was going to be too much for him, they did not want to embarrass him.

I explained I knew the person they were referring to and had always found him to be an honest and dedicated worker, but I had not realized he was a graduate. I suggested there was no reason not to ask him to be a leader in the Classes' initiative, since he had earned the right to be asked, even though they were asking the leaders in the Class to commit to a $50,000 gift. They met with their classmate/employee and made the ask. He asked for some time to consider the amount and said he would get back to them in a week's time. Then he thanked them sincerely for giving him the opportunity to participate in this special and important effort. A week later he responded that he would be honored to help in this way.

It turns out that this special man had graduated from Culver, attended college, and then began his career in banking. He had worked long and successfully in his profession until his wife died. He was struggling with this new reality and decided that he needed a change in venue, as it were, to recapture his excitement about life. He asked himself the question of when he was the happiest in his life, with the exception being when he was with his wife. The answer was clear: it was when he was a cadet at Culver. So, he applied for a job working in the Food Service since he recalled the many kindnesses bestowed on him as a young man by the people working in the Mess Hall, and he wanted to be a part of the energy all those young people provided three times a day. He ended up working there for nearly 20 years until his retirement. Culver truly is a special place, and it has a special relationship with its graduates.

Early on, it struck us that nearly all Culver graduates wore their Culver rings. Now, I had a high school ring that I received as a gift at my graduation, and I may have worn it a few times, but for the last 50 years, it has been resting quietly in a box in a bureau. Culver men, and for the last fifty years, Culver women, wear their Culver rings with great pride. These gold rings are beautifully designed with Culver symbols and the graduate's initials, forming a meaningful symbol of loyalty and respect. I was not surprised to learn from our ring vendor, whom we have worked with since 1924, that we had the highest per capita sales of each graduating class among all their prep school and high school clients.

The Culver ring, whether for CMA or CGA, is a symbol of loyalty, respect and commitment.

The Culver rings worn by alumni who graduated as members of the "Greatest Generation" were particularly distinctive because they had been polished smooth by all the years of wear. Their surface looked marble-like and glistened in the light. These emblems of commitment were the first compelling indications of a personal relationship these graduates had with their school. Possibly more impressive were the stories that helped explain the power of the ring.

The first story we heard described an international financial summit to which only seven representatives from around the world had been invited. The alumnus we were meeting with described his sense of pride as he reached out to shake hands with the others at the summit and realized that three others at the meeting also wore Culver rings. He was impressed, but more importantly, he felt as though this would be an honest and fruitful meeting.

The second legendary story we heard from a graduate who, when he was a young recruit heading off to war, was sitting in the back of a transport truck, literally wringing his hands in nervous anticipation of what he was about to experience in battle. He felt a tap on the shoulder, and the man next to him handed him a Culver ring, and then he pointed back down the line of men sitting on benches in the truck. He then saw the man who had sent the ring down the line, smiling at him and giving him a reassuring look. This young man immediately realized he would be all right; he was in the presence of another Culver man. It turned out that the man who passed his ring along had seen his ring, had realized that the other man was challenged by the situation, and wanted him to know he was not alone.

There were other important and symbolic stories that described the deeply personal and endearing relationships Culver's alumni have with their School. One summer graduate shared with us the intimate details of his and his spouse's prenuptial agreement which included three parts: (1) a life in politics; (2) a commitment to having three children; and (3) a further commitment to send all their children to Culver. Another student on exchange from Great Britain described Culver as "the place I didn't know I needed" after her year there; and this student was already an absolute star when she was chosen to represent a high-profile exchange program as a scholarship recipient.

We had seen the outpouring of support and interest at our annual alumni anniversaries, during which our graduates would turn out in droves to rekindle the fires lit during their Culver days and to re-establish their connection with Culver. One of the ceremonies that was particularly heart-warming was the re-enactment of the 50th Reunion Classes' actual graduation ceremony, which was witnessed in front of the entire student body, faculty and staff. They would line up as they had as first classmen (and seniors, for the classes with women) fifty years earlier and process to the graduation field. The Culver Band, colors, corps of cadets, and CGA students were at the ceremony. Then, as their names were read, each graduate would march individually to the Old Iron Gate — the portal through which a graduate would pass, thus symbolizing the passage from boyhood into manhood, from being a student to becoming an alumnus — render honors to the American flag and the Culver colors, salute the Head of Schools, receive a replica of their original diploma, and pass through the Gate to be greeted by the President of

The Culver Academy for Girls, Class of 1972 re-enact their graduation, this time through the Arch, which didn't exist during their time (it was inaugurated in 1975).

The Culver Legion, just as they had done as young men. Many had tears in their eyes as they made the journey back in time.

One particularly inspiring and telling story we watched play out involved a member of the Class of 1949 who had attended Culver for 3.25 years but had not graduated because of the onset of polio early in his senior year. In those days a case of polio meant quarantine, so this young man was rushed to the hospital in his hometown to deal with the disease. He did not return to finish the year, so he never graduated. He believed erroneously that the school had dismissed him because of the polio, and his parents never explained to him that they wanted to keep him at home for health and safety reasons.

When the Class of 1949 was due for its 50th Reunion — their Golden Anniversary — they asked him to join them for the celebration. He was unaware that they had arranged months earlier with the Academy for him to receive his diploma, based on his record before his departure and his distinguished accomplishments as a professional during his life. I had the honor of awarding him his Culver diploma, and he was completely overwhelmed by the gesture. This was as successful a person as you could imagine, but he was speechless at the moment he realized that his school had never abandoned him and still cared enough to make things right at this propitious moment. He could now wear his Culver ring with pride.

It was not unusual for members of a Reunion Class to come forward on the occasion of their 25th or 40th or even 50th Reunion to ask the Academy to consider awarding

The CMA 50th year class re-enact their graduation ceremony, symbolizing their transition from boyhood to manhood. The Golden Reunion's Iron Gate ceremony is often a powerful and emotional experience, even so many decades later.

a diploma to a classmate who, because of special circumstances like the one above, had not received or qualified for his prized Culver diploma. Some involved classmates who had been unable to finish their course of study due to financial reasons; and some had left Culver because of personal reasons. In all cases the young men had lived exemplary lives and had contributed to and enriched society — they had lived their lives as good Culver men.

Each of these stories was compelling, and the act of presenting each qualified non-graduate his diploma was both gratifying and emotional.

The one I wished I had been able to grant but did not was possibly the most compelling because of the values the experience represented. Almost from the moment we arrived at Culver, members of a particularly impressive and engaged class explained to me that they had a classmate who had not been awarded his diploma because he had gone off to war. There was, of course, a provision for veterans to earn their diplomas upon their return, but this important member of their class still had not received his. They were giving me early warning that as their 50th Reunion approached, they would be asking the Academy to present him with this symbol, which was long overdue.

I was so eager to right this obvious wrong that I contacted their classmate — a man whose military record and whose entire adult life had been filled with acts of honor and achievement — to give him the good news that after all these years he had been approved for his diploma, and that I would be awarding it to him at the celebration of his 50th Reunion. A few days later I received a letter from him thanking me but explaining why he could not possibly accept the diploma. He wrote that when the young men of Culver went off to war, they were told very explicitly that they would qualify for their diplomas only if they entered college upon their return, completed their courses of study and maintained at least a B average. They also would be expected to have excellent citizenship records as college students.

He did all the above, he explained, except after the war he was less industrious in the classroom than he should have been and only earned a C+. His rationale for turning down the school's offer, he reasoned, was that at Culver he had learned to be honorable and accountable for his actions. He added that, if he accepted a diploma, knowing he had not met the full requirements for it, he would be de-valuing the Culver diploma and he would never do that to this school.

I could fill this volume with stories of the deep devotion and the love so many of Culver's graduates have for their school. Some may think this is a natural outcome of the boarding school experience, but having spent thirty years at another boarding school with its own 50th reunion celebration and traditions, I can assure you the Culver connection is significantly different. Probably it is a function of Culver men and women having achieved something significant in the face of demanding and personally challenging circumstances as students and "campers." When you graduate from Culver, you know you have earned a diploma that truly means something. This boarding school diploma is not a rite of passage because of who you are; it is an honor you earn because of what you did. It is not a point of pride that you can use as evidence of how special you are; it is a reminder of how honorable and responsible you were and are expected to be throughout your life.

Recently, I was advising a young head of school about his crafting of a policy to help them eliminate non-payment on tuition bills in the last year of a student's time at their school. They had really never had issues before, but this year they had a few families who balked before making their final payment. I asked him what incentives or consequences they had used once the person-to-person persuasion had failed, and he explained that they threatened to withhold the transcript.

I was surprised for two reasons: withholding a transcript is unlawful, but, more significant, at Culver the most important record a student or his or her family covet is their diploma, never their transcript. Culver really is different. In fact, while we were at Culver, I had the opportunity and the honor to award diplomas to graduates who had earned their diplomas by putting themselves on self-regulated payment plans that lasted 12 to 15 years, just so they could claim that highly-prized piece of paper — it meant that much to them.

An even more compelling warrant for the claim that Culver alumni/ae have the deepest respect for and commitment to their school is the fact that while we were at Culver, at least three alumni founded schools modeled on the Culver system; two others founded schools because of the importance of education to them given their Culver experiences; and three more rose to the leadership ranks of schools serving underserved children and young people using programs and philosophies learned at Culver.

The real difference was never more clear to Pam and me until we participated in the By Example Campaign. I remember well the conversation I had had with some leaders on the Board during the interviewing process. The head of the Finance and Investment Committee asked me what I thought of the financial picture at Culver. At the time I was the CFO/COO of an extremely well-endowed school, arguably the best endowed school in the continental U.S. on a per student basis. That school's endowment was roughly three times the size of Culver's, so on a dollar-to-dollar basis there was no comparison.

Furthermore, my first impression had been that Culver was serving nearly 50 percent more students and providing more programming with many fewer resources. My response was measured, but my analysis was clear: "You are driving a Ferrari, but it is powered by a Volkswagen engine." The Board member's reply was immediate: "That is my analysis as well. What would you intend to do about that reality?" I replied, "We will use wisely the assets and resources we have, and when the time is right, I will come back to you and ask you and others who care deeply about the School to assist us in putting a more appropriate engine in this vehicle." His response was once again succinct: "Agreed."

Five years later, after the collapse of the "tech bubble," after the Iraqi War and after three and a half years of zero gains in the stock market, the Board decided that it was the time to upgrade the engine that had been driving the Culver experience. They set the goal for the By Example Campaign at $200,000,000 and agreed that the quiet phase (before the official announcement) would focus on the first half of the total to be raised.

This was a big number, but it was not an unheard of amount in the boarding school world. That said, only one school had raised that amount, and it was widely understood that the school had "crawled to the finish line" in their campaign, having to depend heavily on many people who had already given earlier in order to get over the top. Surprisingly, when the campaign consultant we had asked to meet with the Board to advise them on the feasibility of Culver's being successful in this historic venture informed us how challenging the goal was, the Chairman of the Culver Board explained to the consultant that we were confident about raising that amount and more.

"Remember, this is Culver." he said. "And, furthermore, we will not be running a conventional campaign in which a few people lead the effort. Nearly all our Board members went to Culver; they know how to lead and to get things done; and each will have a leadership role in the actual campaign."

The consultant was stunned.

"That is not an efficient way to manage a campaign of this size," continued the consultant. "I understand that this is Culver, but all campaigns are similar with regard to organization."

"Not this one!" Jim Henderson added, smiling.

The newly named Campaign Chairman, Miles White '73, the CEO of Abbott Laboratories, reinforced the confidence in the Culver alumni body expressed by the Board Chairman:

"We expect we will surpass this initial goal quickly and reset it higher very early in the process."

The rest, as they say, is history. Remember that Jim Henderson had earlier run a successful $409,000,000 campaign for Princeton University, before taking on the role as Chair of the Princeton board. He was experienced and had participated in and led two remarkably successful campaigns for Culver a decade ago and the two decades before. More importantly, he was as motivated as a person could be. This was personal.

Culver was a family affair for the Henderson family.

He also had a team of Culver Trustees for whom the effort was also personal. Miles White was a son of Culver, his relationship dating back to his arrival at the Academy as an 8th grader. He was one of the only five-year men on the Board, and he had been

The White-DeVries Rowing Center, dedicated in 2012, gave Culver an Olympic-quality facility to match the strength and longevity of its longstanding crew/rowing program.

successful in every aspect of the Culver program — academically, athletically, and as a cadet leader. Miles would chair this effort and would be another great leader By Example. They were now ready to "capitalize" their school. Just as the Culver family had done for their school in its early years, the Culver Board was now stepping up to assure the future of their beloved Academies.

The $200 million-dollar Campaign goal was announced shortly after that meeting, the "quiet phase" goal having been achieved in nearly record time; and almost before the Campaign buttons were made, the Board raised the goal to $300,000,000 — an unheard of number for a secondary school. But this was Culver. When all was said and done, the school raised $376,200,000, and, also unprecedented, had raised 85% of the money for endowment. The construction project dollars totaled $24 million for the new Riding Hall and Stables (raised almost exclusively by Troop alumni and their families); the completely retrofitted Eppley Auditorium for music, drama, and dance; the creation of a state-of-the-art Crew facility funded by two Trustees who had rowed at Culver and had gone on to be successful college oarsmen; and the retrofitting of the former Science Building for use as the new Art Center. The lion's share of the Campaign funds was for financial aid programming—probably the most important dollars any school can secure.

These Culver graduates were not interested in having their names on buildings as a result of this effort; they were interested only in lifting up the name of their beloved Academies. One of the leadership donors was adamant about not having his name placed anywhere on the campus, and only after considerable discussion did he agree to having his name placed on a boulder on one of the campus walkways. His argument was that this was not about him and that he was "only paying the Academy back for what it had done for him as a young man."

The experience of being involved in the By Example campaign was magical. We had a development team only a quarter of the size of the largest and most prosperous schools on the East Coast, but we never felt undermanned in the effort. I remember thinking, as we agreed to undertake this lofty goal, that with the leadership we had, with all the Trustees on board, with the team we had in place, with our alumni/ae energized as they were, and with the future of the Academies at stake, there was no way we could fail. I could never have imagined how educational, uplifting, and joyous a journey this would be. We had the right message, the best traveling companions, and a more than capable and willing group of fans to cheer us on and support us — our alumni, families, and friends.

Among the visible projects enhancing Culver's campus in the 2000s was the Gable Tennis Center, which includes 15 outdoor and five indoor courts.

Looking back on the By Example Campaign with 20/20 hindsight, I am surprised that we had so much confidence in our prospects for success. We had just come through one of the least productive periods in the financial markets in over two decades. The bursting of the "tech bubble" and the War had quelled any notions of improvement in the market, and there were no gains to be had by investing. Announcing a capital campaign in 2003 was not ideal, and ending the Campaign in 2010, having had to survive the worst recession in modern history with the financial collapse in 2008-2009, made the timing more than challenging and among the least conducive for success of any major effort in philanthropy since the 1970s. Except for one important factor, Culver's most successful graduates were not dependent on fee income from the financial markets. They built things; they had ownership positions in their companies; and they were willing to sacrifice deeply for the school that had helped make them who they were.

The vigorous appreciation for history and character among Culver alumni undergirded the restoration of Culver's 1920s golf course, whose original designers, William Langford and Theodore Moreau, were internationally acclaimed. The project included construction of an elegant new golf house and catapulted Culver's course to ranking in the top three 9-hole courses in the world.

They had been trained to lead and to serve. It was not about them; this was for their school. And this was true not only for Culver's American graduates. Culver's close partner in this venture was Mexico, a country that graduated its first Culver alumnus nearly 100 years before we arrived and had seen thousands of its boys and girls, young men and young women attend and graduate from Culver over the next century. Culver was described to us by our younger alumni as the "business card of Mexico," primarily because so many business leaders for Mexico were notably Culver graduates — from both Summer and winter school programs.

One of the lessons of the campaign was the sense that by giving to Culver, people were paying their school back for all it had done for them in their formative years. Maybe it was the symbiotic relationship the alumni/ae had with Culver...as Culver prospered, they prospered, at least psychologically. The Culver experience engendered a sense of confidence in its graduates, and it was that confidence — never arrogance — that propelled them forward in their careers. It takes confidence to take the long view in your business and accept short-term losses to secure long-term benefits for your employees and shareholders, even when others are demanding more immediate profits. It takes confidence to start a new business. It takes confidence to lead companies and not-for-profit Boards and to lead campaigns, when thousands of people are depending on you. Culver's alumni/ae were confident in a way I had never seen before in my career (and I had been involved in campaigns before at an excellent school with well-heeled alumni). This was clearly not a Midwestern thing; it was a Culver outcome.

Here are a few of the special examples of devotion, commitment, and service that helped me understand even more fully why Culver's mission produced the quality of people with the growth mindsets these graduates possessed:

- One alumnus offered to provide a truly significant amount of money as a commitment to a matching effort, stipulating that the match would be applied only to those donations coming to the Academy that were contributed to Culver (not just pledged) to the endowment or the Annual Fund, a gesture he believed would help Culver continue to build its much-needed endowment and also sustain the momentum of the Campaign during the recession and collapse of 2008. This was a time when most schools and colleges suspended their fund-raising efforts. Note: CASE (The Council for the Advancement and Support of Education) wrote the following about this matching gift:

   The Grand Gold Award:
   The Culver Academies — The Batten Leadership Challenge

   The Batten challenge blew us away. Announced in December 2008 when everyone in education was worried about huge losses to our endowments and concerned that our major donors might turn away from this critical gift priority, Culver Academies' brave, counter-cyclical initiative succeeded in building the institution's endowment from $152 million to $280 million in just over one (economically tumultuous) year. The Batten Challenge embodies one of the key elements of Culver's stated Mission: Leadership.

- A very recent graduate sent in his first paycheck and signed it over to Culver as a By Example Campaign donation.

- Another extremely generous and thoughtful alumnus, a member of the Board of Trustees, decided to endow a fund he referred to as a "perma-debt" endowment to assist young faculty coming to the Academies with the payment of their student-loan debt. Since student loans had become such an attractive way of financing a college education, many recent graduates were overwhelmed by their level of debt. He had read that student loan debt was especially challenging for young teachers when it came to paying down their loans, so he came up with a plan. His fund would pay off up to $15,000 of debt for young teachers who spent at least three years teaching at Culver, and he would front end the payment to ensure some immediate financial relief.

- I received a call from an older graduate who had just experienced a heart attack in a mini-marathon and told me that as he rode in the ambulance, he was struck by the three things he committed to doing if he were to survive. Two of them concerned time and quality of interaction with his family, and the third was paying back Culver for all it had given him…so maybe all three were about family. His gift was generous and enabled Culver to endow a program for entrepreneurial studies and practice, something this graduate had modeled in every one of his career endeavors.

- In response to the Batten matching gift offer, one alumnus who was in the middle of paying off a significant five-year pledge for a major leadership gift for endowment, asked for permission to suspend the schedule of his five yearly payments and substitute an additional payment in the same amount to take advantage of the matching opportunity. He assured Culver that he would still make the missed payment the following year, but that this opportunity was too important for Culver to miss. He wanted to honor the donor and he was excited about using the extra payment and match to endow a renovated lecture hall in the name of Jim Henderson's wife, a person who had been with Jim every step of the way as they supported and helped develop Culver.

- This same alumnus and his family also made a special gift to the Academies when they commissioned and delivered to the school an exact replica of the original cutter number 13 which was used to rescue so many citizens during the Logansport flood. This cutter is now used by the Academies as a reminder of the virtues and values of Culver that helped those brave young men to be successful in the rescue effort. Also, it serves as a symbol of the importance and impact of the summer schools and Camps.

- Then a younger alumnus called to say that even though his financial conditions were terrible, he had been inspired by the alumnus who made the matching grant and said he would find a way to make a significant contribution to endow faculty salaries — a remarkably helpful and practical gift — and wanted to go on record that he planned to be the next significant donor to lead future campaigns the way the alumnus offering the match was doing. This was more leadership and service — By Example, at work.

- Board members funded endowments for scholarships first and then added resources to fund programs close to their hearts. One funded a youth minister position so the students in that faith group could be supported personally in their pursuit of their faith traditions. Another created a program that would enable students to travel to Chicago to experience the cultural performances — plays, concerts, special films, art exhibits, and even opera — in that special city. He and his wife, always a full partner in his trusteeship and his philanthropy, named the initiative "Culture in Chicago," and hundreds of students have benefitted from this couple's vision and generosity. Another funded a series he named "Executive Leadership Series," through which he enabled Culver students to hear from people who had accomplished remarkable leadership feats — like summiting the seven highest mountains on the world's seven continents.

- Maybe the most notable statistic from the campaign was the percentage of funds donated by former and current members of the Board of Trustees. All campaign consultants agree that the Board members of all not-for-profit institutions need to be depended upon to raise significant funds in a campaign. I believe that raising 25 percent to 30 percent of the campaign total from one's trustees is considered an excellent result and a positive indication of a board's engagement and loyalty to the organization. Culver's trustees were responsible for 70 percent of the total raised — totally unprecedented, especially in a campaign of this magnitude.

Once again, and unbeknownst to me, I was in the process of being educated about Culver in every aspect of this campaign. My learning curve began when Jim Henderson asked me to write a Case Statement for the campaign. My first thought was that I was possibly the least appropriate person to speak for Culver in this historic undertaking, since I had only been in the Head of Schools' seat for a relatively short time, especially given the long and storied history of the Academy. I took pen to paper, literally, in an effort to be as thoughtful, careful, and visionary as I could be, especially since I still had very little sense of how our Culver alumni/ae would respond to this challenge. I trusted the individuals I had come to know, but I was still learning to trust Culver. Although I had seen this script played out in another school, accomplishing this at Culver was going to be different.

Annual ceremonies like Dean England Day, held each autumn to commemorate the memory and vision of CGA founding dean Mary Frances England, not only point Culver students back to a shared legacy of the past, but immerse them in meaningful and memorable traditions that continue to resonate into their adult lives.

I was surprised how easily building the case came to me. My "Why Culver" declaration was reasonably helpful to the communication consultants who prepared the Campaign materials, I believe, primarily because I had the advantage of complete objectivity as well as an educator's perspective. By the end of the Campaign, however, I understood that the only way I could have been in a position to support the Campaign as fully as I did was to have helped create the context for it. Jim Henderson understood that the best way for me to understand and own the case for this Campaign was to create the first draft. He was once again leading me to ask the right questions in order to reach the best conclusions. He knew that developing the first draft would give me the personal commitment I would need to participate in the effort fully and with the confidence I would need to be a successful leader in the Campaign. This was another important leadership lesson I had learned from Culver and an example of another Culver graduate's leadership acumen.

(Note: at almost the same time Culver was executing the strategy for its momentous By Example campaign, another high-profile eastern boarding school known for its fund-raising expertise ran a $300-million-dollar campaign and ended their efforts with an eye-popping $352,000,000 raised. No one believed that number could be eclipsed by a secondary school. Obviously, they did not remember that the same had been said in the early 1980s when Culver had set the previous record for a campaign by raising $60,000,000 and trumping the efforts of that other iconic boarding school, this one in Massachusetts. Not that Culver is that competitive, but it was an opportunity to show the boarding school world the power of the Culver difference).

One of Culver's most hallowed traditions, dating to the early 20th century, is the Officer Figure, a component of the elegant Final Ball, which takes place each Commencement weekend. The Figure is a highly formal and symbolic set of movements which includes honoring cadet officers' mothers and dates.

Chapter Sixteen: The Case for Culver

In many ways the challenge of making the "case" for Culver transported me right back to our first visit to Culver, to our talks with trustees, and to my work on the dissertation proposal statement, outlining a plan to align the power of the Culver Mission with the marketplace's response to such a relevant, educational institution. I realized I had heard the answer to "Why Culver?" hundreds of times in just our first few years. Current students, alumni, faculty and staff, and retirees (especially people like John Mars, Chan Mitzell, Bob Hartman, Bob Reichley, Peggy Gimbel, Anne Duff, and Janet Stannard Kline) had regaled us with the wonders of Culver. We had met the great classes of Culver, but we began to realize that what we had been told by the classes of the 1970s — there may have been times when there were issues in society that made being a military school more challenging to appreciate, and when the administration of the Academy was struggling to provide the leadership it needed and expected — but the students still loved their classmates, their faculty, and, most importantly, their school. Any person who had experienced Culver, regardless of the program you were involved with — Naval School, School of Horsemanship, Summer School for Girls, School of Aviation, Woodcraft Camp, Culver Military Academy, or Culver Girls Academy — could give you the answer, if you were willing to listen or could hear and digest the answer. I went back to what I had learned from these multiple conversations and from the research I had done.

In one of my early addresses to alumni, families, and friends while we were traveling around the country, I attempted to answer the "Why Culver?" question with the following comments:

- Why would a New Englander, born and bred, and his wife journey from New England to the cornfields of Indiana?

- Why do 36 trustees — men and women of influence and people with unreasonably busy schedules — donate their time and energy so selflessly to support their high school?

- Why do the alumni/ae of these Academies feel so strongly about their School that they make the pilgrimage back to Alumni Weekend at regular intervals for a lifetime?

Because…

- It is a school that had its students grace the pages of USA Today and the Wall Street Journal in the course of one week recently — one for her work as an example of technological inventiveness (entrepreneurship) and the other for his work as a sniper on a peace-keeping mission in the Mideast.

- It has produced and continues to produce people who lead in business, in sports, in entertainment, in law, in education, and in medicine; as well as in families, communities, and in life, in general.

- In a world as uncertain as ours, society needs people who have been educated for responsible citizenship and accountability, who are alert and aware, and who are self-disciplined.

- We cannot afford to have too many Enron scandals in our lifetimes; we need ethics and honest leadership to win the day.

- It's a school with students who live by a Code of Conduct that promotes hard work, honesty, and service to others.

- It has great facilities that provide perfect environments in which to teach a worthwhile mission.

- It has the best, most purposeful, and most exciting and unique Summer Camp in the world.

- It has a Woodcraft program in the summer and curriculum developed by the best minds of the day that continue to evolve in a positive mission-driven manner.

- It sits on the shores of beautiful Lake Maxinkuckee.

- It has a Cavalry — summer and winter, the largest of its kind in the United States.

- It features the Arch and the Iron Gate.

- It has an impressive Color Guard.

- It counts five Medal of Honor recipients among its alumni.

- It responded more sensibly and creatively to the coeducation question than any all-boys school in the United States.

- It has a Prefect system that teaches leadership for girls.

- It reviews its programs annually during Culver Annual Review (C.A.R.) and Culver Women's Celebration (C.W.C.).

- It has meaningful Honor Codes and Honor Councils.

- It has a John Mars.

- It remembers and it celebrates its Gold Star men.

- It has a meaningful and solemn Veterans' Day Ceremony.

- It has "eyes right," even for Butterflies.

- It has Butterflies and Cardinals.

- It has Beavers and Cubs.

- It has a Drum and Bugle Corps.

- It has Garrison parades and the Band's Riposte.

- It has significant alumni who make great sacrifices to support the school's mission.

- It has celebrated a centennial, and it will undoubtedly celebrate another and more.

- It could be the shined shoes…or the made bunks and beds…or learning about yourself in ranks.

- It has the consistency of the experience in CMA and CGA.

- It has alumni/ae who impress you with their humility, their good intentions, their leadership, and their courage.

- It has dedicated and talented faculty.

- It has now and in the past many legendary coaches.

- It provides challenges of the first order.

- It provides opportunities for excellence.

- It provides support to do what's right…always.

- It's a small world and this school plays a big part in it.

Culver is clearly and proudly the only school in the United States, and probably in the world, that has identities as a summer school, a summer camp, a military prep school, and a leadership school for girls. It also celebrates its history and traditions more effectively and regularly than any other place we know. In addition, Culver has the litany of programs, principles, and people like those listed above that serve as warrants for the school's claims of excellence and importance.

Culver may also be the only school in the world to earn a #1 ranking in the national high school athletic polls in hockey and lacrosse.

Therefore, when I sat to write this case statement, I began in the following way:

> Located in the middle of the cornfields in Indiana, this unlikely oasis brings together a quality faculty and staff on a beautiful campus to educate students from all walks of life who share an excitement about their futures. The system is simple and direct: young people learn important lessons for life when the challenge is high, the routine is clear, and accountability is required. Mix in the ceremony and structure of the military system, the leadership opportunities provided for the girls in the Prefect system, the traditions of a century of experience, and the commitment to student leadership, and you have a galvanizing experience and an institution worthy of support. Culver changes lives. Culver transforms capable and motivated boys and girls from adolescents with limited personal resources into young adults prepared to succeed in a competitive and uncertain world — people of character.

> Culver is an important and challenging training ground for future leaders, as important and strong as it has ever been. We have a positive momentum that results from the efforts of many outstanding people. Our recent success in building our physical plant, securing outstanding students, and attracting talented and committed faculty and staff to the campus, position us perfectly for another renaissance. Our recent curricular reforms put Culver at the forefront of secondary education. And our summer camps have never been stronger or more representative of the Culver ideal. Students, faculty, curriculum, and buildings are all in place. Only one piece is missing…an endowment to help ensure a long and sustainable future.

This introduction was intended to inform our alumni that we as a school are as sound and secure as we had been throughout the school's history. Everything I had learned in my research on Culver, and all that I had learned in our first three years on the job led me to two important conclusions: We had a Mission worth keeping, and we had a system that prepared young people for the tasks of adulthood that all educators agreed were necessary for success in the 21st century. At Culver, young people were learning the habits of responsible citizenship and leadership which line up perfectly with virtues and values that lead to a life of personal responsibility and accountability.

Booker T. Washington said, "Few things can help an individual more than to place responsibility on [a person] and to let [that person] know that you trust him [or her]." Unfortunately, there are precious few schools today that place real responsibility on their students. Of course, their students are responsible for the aspects

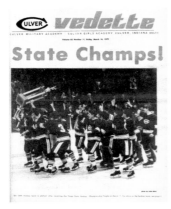

Culver's student newspaper, *The Vedette*, celebrates the first of an ongoing plethora of state hockey championships, in 1979. Similar to lacrosse, Culver's hockey program is consistently ranked top in the nation and has produced numerous NHL players and Olympians — somewhat unexpected for a school in the cornfields of the Midwest.

of the program that involve them, like their academic performance or their athletic performance; but rarely does a student have responsibility for the well-being of others in the school. Some might argue that most schools have adopted a community or public service requirement as part of the curricular programming, a duty that often involves visiting and serving at soup kitchens for the underserved in local communities. Other schools have evolved beyond the requirement of putting in an obligatory number of hours "helping the poor," and have changed the requirement into the formulation of a project with the goal of betterment for a community…not unlike a Boy Scout's Eagle project. There still are very few places that require their students to invest in the well-being of their own school communities, on a daily basis, to serve those around them regardless of their level of need.

There is no question that Culver's mission is dependent on not only ethical training but also practical application. You cannot learn to play the viola by reading a book about the viola; you need to practice it. Where do young people learn their most important lessons and habits about personal responsibility and trust? They learn them by doing. They learn from real life situations, and Culver has made an art form out of training leaders and responsible citizens for our world by giving them that practical training every day in their systems. Furthermore, all the ceremonies, practices, responsibilities, and programs I listed above as possible answers to the "Why Culver?" query are examples of the teaching and training that help develop the sense of confidence, self-efficacy, and personal responsibility exhibited by so many of our graduates.

Students honoring in a given subject present their work before a faculty panel. This CGA student is explaining her Honors in Visual Arts work.

So many alumni/ae have explained to me that the people they are today, the successes they are enjoying today, and the sense of accountability and personal responsibility they embrace as adults began at Culver. Many will say, "I cannot believe how much of who I am I owe to Culver." In fact, recently, a large group of recent graduates met during the Reunion Weekend to share their stories of life after Culver, and the predominant theme of the conversation among this enormously accomplished group of people was the resilience they possessed because of their Culver training. They agreed that Culver taught them never to give up, regardless of the obstacles put in their way. I was reminded of John Mars telling the faculty and students of Culver during that first Convocation when he welcomed us to Culver, that at Culver we will learn to live the words that made Winston Churchill so famous and important in World War II, "Never give in, never give in, never give in!" We have all learned that in the creation of lasting cultures and values, nothing happens by accident. Lasting cultures are created intentionally.

Epilogue

How does a relationship begin? What makes an experience or a series of experiences so meaningful that they stay with you for a lifetime? Why do so many successful people, people with incredibly busy lives, take the time to stay engaged in their school? Why do people who have been recognized publicly for their accomplishments still value recognition from Culver so highly? Remember the Woodcraft dress coat hanging in the closet? Why is it that when you walk into the offices of so many Culver graduates, they have significant Culver memorabilia on display? Are they simply proud of the school from which they graduated or do these mementos serve as important reminders to them of the virtues and values they learned at Culver and carry with them through life?

Most of us recall the situations or the experiences that helped define or refine our characters. Then there were the people who served as mentors and examples for us to follow. Culver people are no different, except that, in addition to the places and people and the particular experiences that they happened upon, they had the benefit of a truly intentional program that introduced them to a set of experiences and exemplars which would serve to teach them habits of heart and mind that would buttress them and inform their most important decisions throughout their lives. Be assured these life lessons go far beyond making one's bed daily…or folding one's clothes in precisely the same way…or making certain one's shoes are well-polished. These are only the indications that the habits have been formed, and they are only symbols of the lessons learned or the character that was formed.

As I was sorting through my mail one day, I came to a small square box, carefully wrapped. When I opened it, I realized it contained a small jewelry box; and inside the box was a Gold C pin from Woodcraft and a hand-written note. The note explained that this Woodcraft graduate was returning his Gold C pin (which meant the world to him) because of a conversation he had had recently with his 10-year-old son. The boy had misrepresented himself in a situation and had taken credit for something he had not actually accomplished himself. The father was deeply concerned that his son would not have the integrity he believed he had modeled for him and gave him a more than stern lecture about misrepresenting a situation. As the father thought about the sternness of the conversation, he thought about the Woodcraft jacket hanging in his closet and the Gold C pin featured among the medals and badges he had earned. Only then did he recall that he had been so consumed with achieving his Gold C pin that he took credit for some work he had not completed, work which qualified him to get the pin.

Shamed by the realization, he retrieved the pin, packaged it up, and sent it back to Culver, explaining he had not met the criteria for a Gold C award; and that he was sorry. My feeling was that if he had not had the proper perspective or values as a young boy in the Woodcraft Camp, he certainly was showing his true character now by admitting his mistake and taking personal responsibility for it. Maybe that's part of the answer to my question.

During our 17 years at Culver, Pam and I had so many conversations, experiences, and personal relationships with Culver graduates that answered the "Why Culver?" question for us, again and again. Our refrain was, "That's why we are here." Whether it was the pride we took from seeing our students perform under the most demanding conditions and in the most demanding circumstances — such as riding down Pennsylvania Avenue in Washington, D.C. or performing in front of thousands of people at the World Equestrian Games in Lexington, Kentucky — or the wisdom and courage they showed as leaders of their respective schools (CGA, CMA, the Naval School, or Woodcraft Camp) on a daily basis; we understood the importance of this place.

Broadway and film legend Josh Logan, class of '27, as a cadet and during one of his several visits to campus, speaking at Culver and interacting with students.

Whether it was the leadership our graduates demonstrated as college students in their respective colleges and universities leading teams, student bodies, or important programs and initiatives, or the impressive record of our graduates as leaders in every walk of life, we saw the value of a Culver education daily. We loved the fact that one of our graduates won the Hobey Baker Award for the best player/sportsman in college hockey one year. We were thrilled that a Culver graduate led the Army Corps of Engineers in the task of "turning the lights on in Baghdad" after the first battle in the War on Iraq.

Whether it was learning about the record of public service our alumni/ae had performed, or their service to our country, or their influence in making significant national policy as politicians, we understood quickly that Culver's educational mission of teaching and learning for self and others makes a difference in your level of engagement with your world.

How many people know that Josh Logan, CMA Class of 1927, Woodcraft Camp 1920–'21; and Summer Naval School 1926; shared a Pulitzer Prize with Rodgers and Hammerstein for co-writing and directing the Broadway hit, *South Pacific*; or that he also directed *Annie Get Your Gun*, *I Married an Angel*, *On Borrowed Time*, and *Mister Roberts*?

In our first few years at Culver, we met a graduate who was responsible for inventing the modern football helmet. Only a few months later we met one of the most renowned hand surgeons in the country…another graduate. Then we were introduced to our Culver Graduate of the Year, who happened to be a famous neurosurgeon who had done the brain research that informed much of the cutting edge, educational practice today. His message to the students was take personal responsibility for the matters that interest or upset you and know that your voice and actions will make a difference — a great Culver message and one very much akin to the one we heard from the West Point Regimental Commander who had graduated 70 years later.

Our responsibilities at Culver led us into relationships with people from every walk of life and stories that never failed to make Pam and me pause to remark: "It must be Culver." For instance, did you know that there were four consecutive years when a World Series-winning baseball team was owned by a Culver graduate: the 1975 (Cincinnati d. Boston), the 1976 (Cincinnati d. New York), 1977 (New York d. Los Angeles), and 1978 (New York d. Los Angeles) World Series? The losing teams — the Yankees and Dodgers respectively — in the last three of these series were also owned by Culver graduates.

Basketball legend Eddie Cameron, CMA class of 1920.

Did you know that the basketball arena/mecca at Duke University, where the "Cameron Crazies" carry on for their team, was named after a Culver graduate in the Class of 1920 who was also one of the founders of the Atlantic Coast Conference? Another graduate used his Culver lessons well and educated himself about all aspects of the America's Cup and won the most prestigious race in yachting. Then he decided to attempt to repeat that feat assembling an all-women's boat — America 3 — and finished second. His formula for success included leadership through teamwork. Sound familiar?

I have told you how many of our graduates — summer and winter — chaired the board of their colleges and universities, were the chief executive officers of Fortune 500 companies, or the presidents of national conglomerates. Even today we continue to hear from our graduates from CGA and CMA that they are often asked how each became such a leader. One CGA graduate was asked by her Stanford professor why it was that everyone else in the class looked to her for leadership and guidance. Her response, "Maybe it's because I went to Culver." Reminds me of the graduate who led the effort to have her university acknowledge Veterans' Day. Do the right thing… always. Give credit where it is due.

America's cup winner and yachting giant Bill Koch '58 returned to campus as Man of the Year in 1992.

In the "By Example" campaign, Culver graduates helped build the Culver endowment to a level of sustainability unimagined when we began the effort. Seven graduates were responsible for creating and funding six individual merit scholarship programs that funded 24 students a year in total and meant that nearly 100 of these merit scholars were in the Academies' student body each year. Add to those hundred students the hundred more who were finalists and semi-finalists in the process and decided to enroll because they and their families saw the exceptional value of a Culver education. At the time they established their programs, their gifts totaled nearly 60 million dollars of endowment for the six programs.

As impressive as that statistic is, once the Campaign was completed, Culver had raised over $200,000,000 in financial aid endowment for traditional financial aid, for special scholarships for middle income families who need but do not qualify for financial aid, and for the merit programs referenced earlier. How's that for honoring the school that helped you become the person who could make such a difference for others? Culver really is about self and others. In the leadership training practicum, students learn to take care of themselves on their journey to learn to take responsibility for and care for others. That is the Culver way.

One of our trustees summited Mt. Everest and planted a Culver flag at the top. Maybe more impressive, he led the effort to revitalize the sport of Skeleton, which returned to the Winter Olympics in 2002.

How many schools' graduates make sure to pack a school pennant when reaching the summit of Mount Everest? Robie Vaughn '74 made it a point during his 2007 climb.

This traditional sledding sport was last seen at the 1928 Games and had gone almost dormant. He provided the leadership, persistence, and resolve, using the creativity, entrepreneurship, force of will, and drive he learned at Culver. The U.S.A. went on to win the Gold Medal in its return to the Winter Olympics stage at the 2002 Salt Lake City Games.

I was talking to an attorney for a Board I was serving on that included a number of Culver graduates, and when he discovered the Culver connection, he remarked that a law partner of his had been particularly impressed by the Chair of the Culver Board who as the CEO of his company had given extraordinary personal attention to a case involving a company employee who had been involved in a serious accident. The partner was amazed that the CEO would take the interest and the time to follow the case as closely as he did. I explained to him that I was not at all surprised since the man he was talking about was a Culver graduate, and Culver alumni understand personal responsibility and empathy well. It's in their DNA. (Remember the Leadership piece citing the importance of emotional intelligence and empathy?)

Pam and I could go on forever touting the virtues of the thousands of Culver alumni/ae we met and came to know well in our seventeen years serving the Academy. We could also cite as many examples of the positive and selfless deeds we witnessed — all indications of the willingness of Culver graduates to have the will to win fairly and the zeal to dare. When Culver students agree to join the Corps of Cadets or receive their Crests as part of their membership in CGA, they agree to follow well and to lead by example; to behave honorably, respectfully, and in a self-disciplined way; to be a good citizen and uphold the Cardinal virtues (Wisdom, Courage, Justice, and Moderation) and the Culver Values (Service, Honor,

Truth, and Duty); to embrace the legitimate traditions of Culver and live well with others; to live by the Culver Honor Code and to treat others with respect and kindness; and by being and becoming the best people they can be. These are behaviors that every educator would aspire to in the education of young people. These are the values of "schools of hope" and "schools of character."

These principles go hand and hand with the tenets of critical thinking, independence of thought, creativity, and the joy of learning. Unfortunately, while many schools offer excellent preparation, they focus on the education of the mind, not the education of the whole person. Doug Heath, author of Schools of Hope, presented his thinking on his definition of "schools of hope" and best practices in education:

> We educate students, not just their minds….Teaching how to take multiple perspectives encourages tolerance and understanding. Educating exclusively for analytical and critical thinking can suppress empathy and sympathy. Nurturing cooperative learning skills and demanding persistence enable the mind's maturation. Snuffing out curiosity and eroding self-confidence impede it."

Heath understood the importance of practice in learning the important concepts of developing a whole person. What can challenge the skills and attitudes of mind more than being responsible for others, working actively with others, and serving others? These are Culver challenges, which ultimately develop self-confidence and nurture cooperative learning skills. This explains why Culver students and Culver graduates are so often chosen or earn the privilege of leading in their schools, professions, and communities. They have the training and the mindset to be confident, grateful, thoughtful, and competent people. It obviously helps when the lessons learned in the classroom are reinforced in one's daily activities and when one is held accountable for his or her actions in both situations.

There is a saying about maintaining a standard of excellence or a high level of performance in matters of the head and the heart: It is like a road that is steep — then you reach the top and you pause to reflect, after which it becomes easy, though it is still hard.

Culver is like that. Culver makes demands on students that few schools make. Starting at the bottom in a new system and then working their way up a ladder of skills and responsibilities until they assume leadership of the system is a challenge. Wearing a uniform or a wardrobe challenges them to be counted as individuals because of what is in their heads and hearts, rather than because of what they are wearing. This is an especially difficult challenge for teenagers. Taking responsibility for others their age or older and younger presents a far bigger challenge, especially when they are 10 years old and those they are responsible for are 10 as well. What makes it bearable and more positive, and eventually reasonable is the building up of habits that make the challenge, while still a challenge, one worth taking on and one that is manageable.

In our last year at Culver, Pam and I were hosting the visit of a longtime Eastern boarding school administrator from what had long been considered one of the most recognizable school names in the country. I had spent most of our meeting trying to explain to him the essence of Culver. I was used to talking about Culver without being fully understood, but since this person was a lifelong school person, I was more hopeful. I smiled when I received an email from him a few days later: "I've been talking about Culver to most anyone who will listen since I got home. The beauty of the setting and buildings, the commitment of the faculty and staff, and the enthusiasm of the students were all striking. More of us, who spent our careers cooped up in New England boarding schools, should see it."

More recently, now that Pam and I have more time to reflect on all that is happening in the world, we hear ourselves saying, surprisingly often, "It's complicated." So much about life is complicated. People have co-opted the expression that something represents a binary choice, but all these issues we face are more involved than simply an either/or choice or solution. There are so many factors that have shaped or contributed to the conundrum we often are trying to sort out. "It's complicated" applies in so many situations, and it occurs to me, it also applies when it comes to Culver.

When I sat down and began writing about our relationship with a school that had formed lasting and impactful relationships with so many people, I imagined there was an easy answer. I had always thought the world was best explained by the lessons of Dorothy in The Wizard of Oz. There is a disruption in her world, followed by a challenge or set of challenges that need to be addressed; there are people she meets along the way who support her and teach her the virtues of wisdom, courage, justice, and moderation; and there are also those who seem to be there to thwart her in her effort to succeed. Nevertheless, she moves forward, since she is looking for the answer, worried that in the final analysis no one can give her the answer or the formula for success. Then she comes to realize she had the answer within her all the time.

Like Dorothy, Culver students are the answer and possess the skills and the strength of character they need because of their experiences with mentors, new friends, family, and the challenges of life. They are up to the task, and all they have to do is assume personal control and individual responsibility for themselves.

Was it possible that this Wizard of Oz metaphor had been with me since we first traveled to Culver? Someone at our former school had asked us upon our return what Culver was like, and I responded:

> It is like The Wizard of Oz. You are traveling through endless fields — in this case corn fields and not poppy fields — and the landscape appears to be relatively free of color, when suddenly you come over the crest of a hill and the campus appears before you, in living color. The setting, the buildings, the lake, the fields and the cabins — appear miraculously before your eyes — moving you from the realm of black and white into full color. It's dazzling.

Then I remembered, as I was writing this text, that I had concluded my second Opening Convocation in August of 2000 in the following way:

> Possibly like you, Dorothy finds herself in a new place, having to fend for herself. She is challenged intellectually, personally, and physically. She has a companion with her, Toto, possibly serving as a symbol of something other than herself that she will need to serve and be

responsible for. She proceeds on a journey that will teach her what she needs to learn to be successful and responsible in life — what we refer to as virtues and shared values. Dorothy's journey — by experience and relationships — teaches her that what she needs in order to be successful, she already possesses. She just needs to develop it, appreciate it, and use it.

Culver has similarities to the Yellow Brick Road. We have our own ladies in funny hats, fields of poppies, and possibly a few individuals whose bark may be bigger than their bite. We have lions, scarecrows, tin woodsmen, and maybe a few wizards. There are horses of a different color and gates that guard the integrity of the Academies. We have parades, pomp, and circumstance, and even a few munchkins — especially in the summer. The journey here is more important than the setting. And finally, I can guarantee you that you will hear yourself more than once saying, "We are not in Kansas anymore, Toto!"

Life will become more complex as you work through the concepts and the conflicts. But the journey will shape who you are and what you will become; it is the vehicle for the process.

Appropriately, at the end of the journey Dorothy tells her new companions that she will never forget them because they taught her so much about life, shared their best with her, and helped her learn and finally understand that she could trust herself to do the right thing. Her relationship with these mentors made her "fit for the future" and, most importantly, not only for her academic future. They had "captured her heart for life in the process." They had given her the tools and attitudes she would need to lead and serve. They were a part of her, just as Culver becomes a part of everyone who processes through the Iron Gate, the Arch, or the summer school portal.

Relationships are complicated. They are formed nearly the same way a person's character is formed. They can be formed through success or adversity. They result from a process involving a challenge, relationships, and in the best of cases, closure. This may explain why Culver has been so important to so many people. It should also serve as part of the explanation of "Why Culver?"

Culver changes one's life because its mission is challenging and demanding and important for young people. The reason people care so much about the well-being of their school; why they believe that Culver is responsible for so much of what they have become in life; and why they carry its ideals with them as their "goal and guide," and are willing to support it with their time and treasure, is complicated, and seems anti-climactic. Nevertheless, it is true. Culver is the secret sauce. Culver is the secret society. Culver may still be the best kept secret in the world, known only to and by those who have experienced its power.

As Pam and I were getting ready to make our farewell address to the school, we were walking along the Lake, just as we had on that memorable first day on the job. This time we were not trying to solve the mystery of the explosion at dawn. We were reminiscing about what we would carry with us from our journey to and from our Oz.

We came upon a plaque that was placed on a boulder near the Lake, and though it was prominently situated, we had never stopped to read its moving message. It turned out that a young Culver man, on the occasion of his graduation from Culver, wrote his farewell message, realizing that he was terminally ill at the time. His words were published first in his Culver yearbook, the Roll Call. It was entitled, "On Saying Farewell to Culver."

Before the day of parting comes, before I take my place among the world of men,

E'er bugles sound their final notes, e'er when the hand of time shall close for evermore,

This chapter of my life,

I'll walk alone recalling memories of happy hours and bid silent farewell to everyone.

These loyal friends I've found, I'll ne'er forget. They'll ever keep my soul alive, aglow with youthful memories.

And when I span the coming years, before my star has set, "I'll stand with pride once more, and say: "I know she sent into the world a Culver man!"

John Lewis Adams '31
October 26, 1911–1931

Culver is a mindset. Culver is a way of seeing the world. The experience of attending Culver reminds you of what it means and what it takes to be your best self. The alumni reading this explanation of their Academy, their School, must understand that it was always clear to Pam and me that we were interlopers, not actual Culver people. We were given the opportunity and the privilege to serve Culver, but we were observers who became converts. The difference is that we had front row seats to the experiences of thousands of young men and women who graduated while we were there and tens of thousands of graduates who were products of Culver. Culver is a wonderful, significant, academically rigorous, personally challenging school with a clear mission and a culture that screams opportunity, responsibility/leadership and service that is healthy and important for young people. And wherever they go in the world, they remember… It's Culver, Culver, Culver… and proud should they all be that they are Culver grads.

Acknowledgments

In retrospect there were many reasons for us to want to be at Culver, and all turned out to be even more compelling the more we experienced and understood the School(s) and their history. Simply put, it was always about the people we met and the friends we made there.

My lieutenant colonel friend who created the decision-making matrix for me as we were weighing the relative strengths of the schools we were considering becoming a part of, was absolutely correct when he highlighted the importance of a "professional" Board of Trustees as the most important factor in our decision. He understood we would not be well served unless we had a group of people who understood the concept of servant leadership; people who would challenge us and partner with us. We were looking for and needing people who "grew" as they took on their stewardship responsibilities; not the ones who "swelled." What we did not understand at the time was that this meant we were looking for Culver people; and that because they were Culver people, they would be what we needed. As was the case with the young lady who spent only one year at Culver as an English-Speaking Union Scholar with us articulated so perfectly, "Culver was the place I didn't know I needed." The people made the difference, and it all began with the Trustees.

As a side note, many schools today struggle with the Board-Head of School relationship. Our former school had moved from a "Greatest Generation" Board when we first arrived to a "Baby Boomer" Board, and the difference was palpable…and not always positive or helpful. From 1969 through 1992 (23 years) we worked with only two Board Chairs, and the Board was a beacon of reason and responsible governance, but in the ensuing 10 years we had changed Board Chairs three times, and in the next decade, the school had three more changes of "leadership." Change may be the only constant, but too much change can destabilize a school. Therefore, stability and mature and responsible, service-oriented leadership are important. Culver had those. In fact, in the last 53 years Culver has had only four Board Chairmen (six in 90 years).

During our time at Culver, we were blessed with two extraordinary Board Chairmen, Jim Henderson and Miles White. They represented different generations and had different experiences with leadership, but both embodied the ideals of Culver. What they shared was a love of Culver and a commitment to doing the right thing for the school. Both "grew up" at Culver, have had children graduate from Culver, and both believe that Culver and its "Giants" helped shape who and what they have become as adults — as husbands, fathers, grandfathers, and business leaders. Like so many "heroes" of Culver, they have the "hope to win and the zeal to dare." Both have led their businesses courageously by making decisions with a long-term view when maintaining the status quo would have been easier and more comfortable for their companies; but they challenge themselves always to do the right thing. They learned about "right action, always" early in life. We could not have had better guides in the process.

We also benefitted greatly from the women and men who served Culver as Board members during our 17 years there. They were the most attentive, most generous, and the most responsible fiduciaries we had ever worked with in the 47 years we have worked with school trustees. From the very beginning of our relationship with Culver, our conversations, meetings, and personal interactions with past and present trustees cemented our commitment to this School and to its alumni. We trusted them almost immediately because these exemplars were in it for Culver. There was no unhealthy ego or self-aggrandizement. There was no vicarious importance associated with their roles as leaders. They represented the wisdom, courage, justice, and moderation every alumnus and alumna at any school or college/university would hope to have as guardians for its institution. We learned from their example.

In the beginning it impressed us and, in some ways, amused us that so many virtuosos graduated from Culver. And we were not easily impressed. The CEOs of Texaco and Corning Glass had chaired the Board of our former School, and they were special people. (Possibly because the Texaco CEO was a graduate of the Naval Academy — another example of military education hardihood and reason!) The Culver Board, by comparison, included the following, just to name a few:

Joe Levy, '43 — *CEO Levy Enterprises*

Frank Batten, '45 — *CEO Landmark Communications and owner of the Weather Channel.*

Charlie Brumbach, '46 — *CEO of the Tribune Company*

Sam Butler, '47 — *Managing Partner of Cravath, Swain & Moore*

Paul Gignilliat, '49 — *Senior V.P. UBS Financial*

Jim Henderson, '52 — *CEO of Cummins Engine Company*

General Jack Woodmansee, '52 — *Three Star General, U.S. Army*

Harry L. Crisp, '53 — *CEO, Pepsi Mid-America*

Larry Wilson, '54 — *CEO of Rohm and Haas*

Jim Dunlap '56 — *President of Texaco*

Bernardo Quintana, '59 — *CEO of ICA (Largest Construction Company in Central America)*

John Ruan, '61 — *CEO of Ruan Industries*

John Zeglis, W'61, NB'64 — *CEO AT&T Wireless (former President of AT&T)*

Craig Duchossois, '62 — *CEO of Duchossois Industries*

Jim Dicke II, '64 — *CEO Crown Equipment Corporation*

Jamie Fellowes, '64 — *CEO of Fellowes Industries*

Ward Lay, '64 — *Pepsi Co. and Frito Lay Enterprises*

Judd Little, '65 — *CEO of the Quentin Little Company*

Todd Parchman, '72 — *Managing Partner of Parchman, Vaughan and Company*

Miles White, '73 — *CEO of Abbot Labs*

George DeVries, '76 — *CEO of AHS—Health Systems*

Dartanian Warr, '76 — *Colonel, U.S. Air Force America domiciled in Mexico*

Additionally, the following had served on the Board just before we arrived:

Jack Warner, '36 — *CEO of Gulf States Paper Company*

Bud Adams, '40 — *CEO of Adams Oil and Gas and Owner of the Houston Oilers/Tennessee Titans*

Cortlandt Dietler, '40 — *CEO of Dietler Enterprises*

Robert Vlasic, '44 — *CEO of Vlasic Pickles and Campbell's Soup Company*

George Steinbrenner, '48 — *Owner of American Shipbuilding and CEO of the New York Yankees*

Greg "Barney" Poole, '53 — *Gregory Poole Caterpillar Equipment Company*

Tom Sullivan, '55 — *CEO of RPM Inc.*

Bill Koch, '58 — *CEO of Koch Industries*

George Roberts, '62 — *KKR Principal/Owner*

Michael Huffington, '65 — *Congressman from California*

This was a "Who's Who" of Fortune 500 companies, and if I included their leadership of university and college boards, that list would be equally impressive. Added to this list of business luminaries are the doctors, scientists, judges, community leaders, and educators whose contributions to Culver's governance issues were equally impactful. It was these people who personified the Culver experience for us and demonstrated the power of the Culver approach. They were generous leaders of character, and they taught us, supported us, partnered with us, and guided us through the process of connecting with our new Schools. Truthfully, part of the motivation for writing this book was to respond thoughtfully to requests from people like George Roberts who wanted there to be a book about Culver that would help answer the question: "Why Culver." They deserve at least my best effort.

Daily, Pam and I used what we learned from the Board — when we were at Culver and now use in retirement. We recall with gratitude being so warmly welcomed to Culver by Jane Doehrman Eberly, CAG '73; Dr. Peggy Riecker Thompson, CGA '77, Jim and Toots Henderson, '52, Paul and Ellen Gignilliat, '49, David and Joan Culver, '59, and Joe Levy, '43. We could not be more grateful to this remarkable group of Culver leaders who believed in Culver, and by extension, taught us to value the school as they did.

This "memoir" contains precious few names of impressive graduates or even those other Board members whose identities are less obvious. I wanted the emphasis to be on what people did rather than who they were. Former President Reagan was famous for reminding people "that it is remarkable how much you can accomplish when you do not worry about who gets the credit." This was an exercise for me in celebrating a group of people who never cared about getting the credit for the support of a special program, the outcome of a legendary campaign, or a thriving school. Selflessness, servant leadership, and leadership keep coming to the fore in these pages and examples.

We were focused in our time at Culver on the relationship between Culver's graduates and their school. We wanted the emphasis to be on the qualities of the place that cemented these relationships and the philosophy that makes Culver such an important player in the educational space today. Any Culver graduate who leads by example works to live the Culver Code of Conduct, and those who lead by seeking first to serve are just as noteworthy to us as any of the examples we highlighted in these pages. That is the power of Culver.